Inside the Vicious Heart

Locations of camps discussed within present political borders

Inside the Vicious Heart

AMERICANS AND THE LIBERATION OF NAZI CONCENTRATION CAMPS

Robert H. Abzug

New York   Oxford
OXFORD UNIVERSITY PRESS

Oxford University Press

Oxford   New York   Toronto
Delhi   Bombay   Calcutta   Madras   Karachi
Petaling Jaya   Singapore   Hong Kong   Tokyo
Nairobi   Dar es Salaam   Cape Town
Melbourne   Auckland

and associated companies in
Beirut   Berlin   Ibadan   Nicosia

First published in 1985 by Oxford University Press, Inc.,
198 Madison Avenue, New York, New York 10016-4314
First issued as an Oxford University Press paperback, 1987

Oxford is a registered trademark of Oxford University Press

Library of Congress Cataloging in Publication Data

Abzug, Robert H.
  Inside the vicious heart.

  Bibliography: p.
  Includes index.
  1. World War, 1939–1945—Concentration camps—Germany.
2. World War, 1939–1945—Prisoners and Prisons, German.
3. World War, 1939–1945—Atrocities.   4. Concentration camps—
Germany—Public opinion.   5. Public opinion—United States.
6. United States—History—1933–1945.   7. Germany—History—
1933–1945.
I. Title.
D805.G3A343   1985   940.54'72'43   84–27252
ISBN 0-19-503597-6
ISBN 0-19-504236-0 (pbk.)

The photographs in this book were supplied by the U.S. Army Signal
Corps with the exception of those with the indication (Witness to the
Holocaust) or (USAMHI).

Quote from *On Photography* by Susan Sontag reprinted by permission of
Farrar, Straus, & Giroux, Inc. Copyright © 1973, 1974, 1977 by Susan
Sontag.

Printing (last digit): 9 8

Printed in the United States of America

to the memory and in the spirit of
Fred Roberts Crawford

Ye that love the Lord, hate evil
Psalm 97:10

Nothing I have seen—in photographs or in real life—ever cut me as sharply, deeply, instantaneously. . . . When I looked at those photographs, something broke. Some limit had been reached, and not only that of horror; I felt irrevocably grieved, wounded, but a part of my feelings started to tighten; something went dead; something is still crying. —Susan Sontag, describing her reaction to the pictures of Bergen-Belsen and Dachau in 1945, in *On Photography*.

Preface

When we think of the major events of World War II, we instinctively turn to the great battles and calamities, the turning points of the conflict: Pearl Harbor, Bataan, Guadalcanal, Iwo Jima, El Alemein, D-Day, the Battle of the Bulge, Stalingrad, and countless others. By comparison in military terms at least the liberation of the Nazi concentration camps in the Spring of 1945 meant little. All the camps were taken easily or with no resistance at all, and none of the liberations hastened what was already an assured victory. In the story of World War II told as the clash of great armies, Dachau, Buchenwald, Nordhausen, Bergen-Belsen, and Mauthausen have no place.

Yet we know these names and the realities they represent. They sit in our consciousness as half-repressed photographs and newsreels, the first images and always present reminders of what is now called the Holocaust: a pile of leathered corpses stacked neatly, as it was said, "like cordwood," or heaped randomly into an anarchy of arms, legs, and heads; close-ups of half-smashed skulls, a last shriek of pain frozen on the faces; the dying, still and vacant, on the ground or on the shelves that passed for beds, beyond the reach of food or medicine; the survivors, eyes dark and deep-set, with wavering skeletons for bodies; bulldozers tumbling limp corpses by the thousands into mass graves.

Most of these scenes were recorded by Allied cameramen at the liberations, and their dissemination in April and May of 1945 marked a turning point in Western consciousness. A visceral tremor passed through those who witnessed scenes of the camps in the darkness of movie theatres or at home in newspapers and magazines. Some cried, some were sick, others were simply stunned to silence. "It was unbearable," remembered Alfred Kazin of seeing the carnage of Belsen at a Piccadilly cinema. "People coughed in embarrassment, and in embarrassment many laughed." The scenes were a double wound for, appalling in their own right, they also confirmed beyond words what two world wars had already suggested—that Western civilization, so satisfied with itself as the flower of human evolution, might still use its vaunted minds and machines to serve the darkest and most primitive impulses.[1]

Forty years later it is hard to imagine that jolting shock, for by now we have become experts in observing misery and in the trafficking of cultural guilt. We know about Auschwitz and Buchenwald. We attach human names to evil and suffering: Adolf Eichmann, Anne Frank, and a train of other perpetrators and victims, each unique in perversion or martyrdom. Not a month goes by without a new corner of Holocaust history illuminated or a new attempt in film or fiction to evoke a vision of its horror. The words are read and the movies viewed within the accepted canons of art and scholarship, their subject matter made a part of our normal vocabularies and emotions. What once seemed impossible has become a benchmark in our moral discourse, a symbol of humankind's expanded capacities for evil.

Nearly absent from this burgeoning literature and dialogue is serious consideration of the moment of discovery itself—the weeks of April and May 1945 when Allied soldiers and reporters opened the camps and revealed the unspeakable carnage that forced us to believe all that had been rumored and all that we would later find out. Even with such eyewitness confirmation, some still deny the Holocaust ever happened and others avoid its reality in a variety of artful ways. Had an accident of history denied British and American soldiers their naked confrontation with the camps, it is reasonable to assume that the Holocaust might have become like the Soviet camps, the Turkish slaughter of the Armenians, or the massacres of Cambodians in Southeast Asia—reported and put out of mind, known and dismissed, prey to every denial or charge of political manipulation.

That may seem an overstatement. Yet imagine the situation if the Nazis themselves had done more to clean up the camps in expectation of Allied advances. They had done exactly that in the case of the Polish extermination camps, and one result was that initial reports coming from Soviet sources in 1944 and early 1945 seemed pale in comparison with the later revelations. What if it had only been the Soviets who overran the camps? With the onset of the Cold War, Soviet sources might well have been held in contempt and, besides, the urge to sanitize the record of our new German allies might have been irresistible. Such trends manifested themselves despite the opening of the camps in the spring of 1945. If those in the West had not seen Belsen and Buchenwald, how much of the record of Auschwitz would have continued to be dismissed as "Hun atrocities" propaganda similar to the "Rape of Belgium" and other inventions of World War I?[2]

What follows is a description and analysis of the experiences of GIs and other American eyewitnesses as they grappled with some of the most frightening scenes in modern history. It is also an attempt to understand the immediate and long-range impact of their discoveries on the public mind. For the liberations are important not only because of the scenes revealed and the men and women rescued. They afford us a window on the way men and women act and think when faced with the unimaginable suffering of others. The deep compassion and sometimes the limits of vision displayed in such circumstances were all in evidence at the camps, and in themselves pointed to important ambivalences about facing the Holocaust and its victims that surfaced immediately after the liberations and for years to come.

This story is told from a number of perspectives. It begins by assessing the range and quality of American belief concerning the camps before the liberations that occurred in the spring of 1945. The chapters that follow turn to the liberations themselves and focus on the experience of Americans actually there. They also recount some of the history of each camp in order for the reader to understand better some of the immediate background of the carnage eyewitnesses confronted. The book then considers the ways in which the story of the camps was transmitted to the American people, and analyzes sometimes surprising reactions to the news. Finally, it explores the problems Americans in charge of rehabilitating and repatriating survivors had in understanding their condition and needs.

We like to think of liberations as noble and heroic events, and those elements were certainly present when the camps were opened. Thousands of men and women who considered their fates sealed were given the chance to build a second life; thousands of liberators gained profound insight into the importance of the war effort. What follows, however, tries to probe more deeply into the ways the liberators managed to face the scenes around them and into the deep pit of awful experience that separated liberator from survivor even as fate joined them at a crucial moment in history.

This book is basically about Americans and their confrontation with the camps. Similar books could and should be written about British, French, and Soviet soldiers and those of a dozen other nations who took part in liberating the hundreds of Nazi camps. I have limited myself to Americans because America is the culture I know best and because any wider study would have been unmanageable. I also do not say much about the reactions of survivors, although in many ways theirs may be the most important drama of all. I think it is a story best told by the survivors themselves, for only they can possibly know (but perhaps even they can find no words to express) the full meaning of these events. I have set for myself the humbler task of recounting and understanding the liberations in the minds of relatively innocent souls, nothing in whose lives had prepared them for their brush with the unfathomable darkness of the camp universe.

In order to come close to that experience, I have combed archives and picture collections, newspapers and magazines, biographies and memoirs, and have called upon the testimony of the liberators themselves. My hope is that the mixture of historical narrative and analysis, first-person accounts, and photographs from both official and private collections will give the reader a vivid sense of how the liberations affected those unsuspecting souls whom historical accident made witnesses to the camps, and how their discovery has affected us all.

Austin, Texas   Robert H. Abzug
September 1984

Contents

Inside the Vicious Heart

1 | A Double Vision

The Vosges Mountains rise suddenly from the Alsatian plain southwest of Strasbourg, a mirror of the German Schwarzwald across the Rhine. Villages and small towns dot the valleys, dwarfed by the dense, dark pine forests that rise above them. In summer the Vosges luxuriate in many shades of warm green, but by late fall they take on the miserable beauty of snow and fog and piercing winds. In November and December 1944, these mountains in all their bitter greyness greeted two armies, the French First and American Seventh; six hardfought months after D-Day, they had cornered German resistance in Alsace into a pocket around Colmar and pushed within striking distance of Germany. As the French army moved through the Vosges around Schirmeck, it discovered a place infamous in the annals of the German occupation. On a bald hillside, up a winding road from the village of Natzwiller and through a tunnel of pines, stood an abandoned concentration camp: Natzwiller-Struthof.

The Nazis built Natzwiller as a labor camp in 1941 to quarry the local red granite for monuments in Germany. Originally the inmates were German, but by 1943 the Nazis expanded the camp's use to the killing of Jews, Gypsies, and captured Resistance fighters from Holland, Belgium, and France. Some died from overwork, while others perished from torture or disease. As the camp took on its new function, a gas chamber and improved crematory were added, and new uses were found for the inhabitants. University of Strasbourg scientists performed experiments concerning treatment of mustard gas wounds. Of 250 prisoners forced to be guinea pigs, fifty died and the rest were tortured and disfigured by the gas and various "treatments." Three hundred prisoners were given typhus to test an anti-typhus vaccine. Similar experiments explored cures for jaundice. Natzwiller also became a source of preserved skeletons from handpicked prisoners, these to populate the Strasbourg Anatomical Institute and anthropological collections elsewhere as specimens of Jews and other "lesser" varieties of humankind. With the approach of Allied troops in 1944 the SS evacuated the camp, and when the French army found it in November it had been abandoned for more than two months. Natzwiller was the first major Nazi concentration camp to be uncovered in the West.[1]

The *New York Times*'s Milton Bracker toured the site in early December. He knew little of Natzwiller's own sordid history, indeed some of the details would not become known until the war crimes trials. Nonetheless Bracker was not an innocent. American newspapers and magazines had reported the existence of concentration camps since early 1933, when Dachau first slammed its gate shut on a group of Communists and other political enemies of the Nazis. Dachau, Buchenwald, and other prewar camps had gained lurid reputations for harsh labor regimes and sadism.

As early as August 18, 1940, a CBS News Berlin correspondent reported a speech by Hans Frank, Nazi governor of occupied Poland, who in announcing plans to make Cracow free of Jews, had added: ". . . and it is clear that herewith, a serious warning must be given—the Jews must vanish from the face of the earth."[2] By 1942, shocking but well-documented stories appeared in mass circulation magazines like *Time, Newsweek,* and the *Saturday Evening Post* that told of slaughter in Poland and other countries and the removal of Jews to labor and death camps. Some estimated that the Nazis had already killed over two million Jews and enslaved millions of others. The American and British governments confirmed these reports, and various Jewish groups and sympathizers among non-Jews vainly sought a way to curb the killings.

Just five months before his own trip to Natzwiller, Bracker knew, soldiers of the Red Army had discovered the abandoned Majdanek extermination camp near Lublin, in Poland. In September 1944, American reporters visited Lublin, and stories featuring pictures of an ominous warehouse bursting with 800,000 shoes that had once belonged to Nazi victims were widely published. The few survivors the Soviets encountered told of the slaughter, and mass burial sites confirmed their stories. So did piles of discarded Zyklon-B gas canisters.[3]

Although the *Times* reporter was aware of this history of Nazi atrocity as he approached Natzwiller, he found it difficult to connect the two. "It might have been a Civilian Conservation Corps camp," he wrote in the *New York Times* of December 5, 1944. "From the winding road to the bald hilltop, the sturdy green barrack buildings looked exactly like those that housed forestry trainees in the United States during the early New Deal." He stood in awe of the "stark wild magnificence" of the setting, snow swirling over the barracks and the hard ground, making faint and eerie its commanding view of distant mountains and the valley village of Rothau below. "One had to force into one's consciousness," he continued, "the fact that this was not a foresters' or lumbermen's camp," that it had been until recently "the charnel-house of the St. Die Valley—the Lublin of Alsace."[4]

Even after Bracker entered the compound through electrified double barbed-wire, he found in the silent emptiness of Natzwiller a kind of innocence. "There were no prisoners, no screams, no burly guards," he observed, "no taint of death in the air as on a battlefield." Bracker entered the crematorium. "I cranked the elevator tray a few times," he reported, "and slid the furnace tray a few times and then realized that, even at this moment, I did not believe that what I was doing was real." His Free French guide then took him to a small dark room with almost fifty S-shaped hooks suspended from metal rods on the ceiling. The guide asked him to hold his wrists together and hang from a hook; Bracker did so, feeling acute pain in his back and kidneys as his heels struggled to touch the ground. The Frenchman told him that prisoners were whipped in this position, and that gas was then pumped into the room to finish them off. Finally, Bracker saw the dissection room, as well as one small storage room crammed with burial urns, some of red clay and some of thin metal.

Barracks at Natzwiller, December 1944.

He wrote all of this as an eyewitness, and left to the end of his story some details that were "necessarily second-hand." "[B]ut it is certain," he added, "that the crematorium, the hooks, the gas orifices, the dissection slab and the urns were not used for mere decoration." Some believed that the burial urns were "simply a commercial touch enabling the Germans to sell them to the victims' families," but he could not "vouch for that." He also had to take the word of the French that 16,000 persons had come as prisoners to Natzwiller between late 1941 and the evacuation in the summer of 1944, and that 4,000 perished.

Bracker's observations were those of an experienced reporter, on one level sure of what he was looking at, yet also fully aware that the connection between the artifacts of Natzwiller and millions dead could not be grasped even on personal inspection. It was hard to connect a crime of such vast proportions to the remains at Natzwiller, yet everything pointed to its being the "Lublin of Alsace." As a good newspaperman, he realized that the gap in

Burial urns at Natzwiller.

American soldier tests crematorium elevator, Natzwiller.

comprehension, that double vision, was as much a story as the fraction of the concentration camp network he had seen.

Less sophisticated readings of the camp were possible: ones that turned disbelief into an undercurrent of doubt, or at least suspended judgment. On December 9, 1944, five days after Bracker had made his tour, Colonel Paul Kirk and Lt. Colonel Edward J. Gully of the American Sixth Army Group inspected Natzwiller. It is impossible to know what they had heard or believed about Nazi atrocities; it is clear they approached their job with caution. In the report they made to headquarters, which was eventually forwarded to the war crimes division, they qualified just about every observation that had to do with instruments of death and torture. They found, among other things, "what appeared to be a disinfestation unit" and "a large pile of hair appearing and reputed to be human female." They were shown a building with a space "allegedly used

9

as a lethal gas chamber." In this building was "a cellar room with a special type elevator," and "an incinerator room with equipment obviously intended for the burning of human bodies . . . a cell room and an autopsy room." Kirk and Gully then described in detail the "so-called lethal gas chamber," noting every pipe and outlet and its two steel doors. In the cellar they found four coffins and a sheet metal elevator "of a size which would take a human body" with "stains which appeared to be caused by blood."[5]

Archaeologists in a modern ruin, Kirk and Gully had all the artifacts in place but nonetheless could not quite put together what they had found. The rational in them observed and touched the camp's hardware and even viewed telltale remnants of Natzwiller's victims. They duly recorded the testimony of French informants and reported their findings. Yet something in them balked. Milton Bracker had observed his own disbelief and understood it for what it was. These American army officers, less introspective perhaps or less knowledgeable about Nazi crimes, simultaneously listened and doubted. They believed enough to send along their report to war crimes investigators, but retained a measure of disbelief. In this sense they were typical of many American officers in France, who sometimes infuriated the local populations by doubting and sometimes even scoffing at stories of German inhumanity.[6]

In many ways the caution reflected in these surveyors of a Nazi ruin reflected a deep strain in every quarter of American opinion concerning the reality of Nazi atrocities. It was not that most Americans did not believe the press reports. In November 1944 George Gallup had asked the nation: "Do you believe the stories that the Germans have murdered many people in concentration camps?" He found that 76 percent believed the stories, only 12 percent did not, and 12 percent had no opinion. However, most found it very hard to imagine the magnitude of human destruction. When asked to estimate the numbers killed, almost 36 percent of those who believed people were being murdered in the camps said deaths amounted to 100,000 or less; just over 50 percent believed the figure to be a million or less; 33 percent had no opinion; while only 16 percent thought that between two and six million or more had died. Thus the majority fell far short in their estimates despite

Autopsy table, Natzwiller.

the fact that the press reports presumably read by these people had correctly numbered the victims in the multi-millions.[7]

There can be no simple explanation of the inability of Americans to imagine the full extent of Nazi atrocities, but one can point to a combination of factors that contributed to this resistance. Many Americans, of course, could not forget that during World War I the government promulgated stories of German atrocities that were later admitted to be complete fabrications. As one American remembered: "I had first heard about the camps by reading about them in the newspapers. I thought it was propaganda put out like the propaganda about Germans' cutting off women's breasts in Belgium and killing children by stabbing them with bayonets."[8]

Storeroom for prisoners' clothing, Natzwiller.

If such stories had been lies twenty-five years before, why should one believe similar reports to be true in 1943 and 1944? Those who rejected stories of Nazi genocide outright often did so on these grounds. For others, the legacy of World War I left lingering suspicions of exaggeration or fabrication when it came to the Nazis. Something bad was happening, they said to themselves, but could one really believe the Germans were literally bent on or capable of exterminating the Jews and enslaving millions of others? It is hard to gauge precisely how influential the "atrocity stories" argument was, but an extraordinary number of pleas, editorials, and reports concerning the camps and related atrocities directly or indirectly felt it necessary to argue against the charge that the latest stories out of Europe were mere propaganda.[9]

No matter how rational or understandable the fear of being duped again by propaganda seems, such an explanation of caution or outright rejection concerning reports of Nazi atrocities masks as much as it explains. It ignores a basic difference in what the public was asked to accept. World War I stories, for the most part, recounted lurid individual acts of sadism and violence. No matter how brutal, these tales did relate at least to a fantasy world that most persons could imagine and to which they could react. Stories of individual sadistic acts were also part of the press image of Germans in World War II. However, the numbers and techniques involved in reports of Nazi genocide pushed one's imagination to the very brink. A policy to annihilate a whole group or enslave a whole nation? Camps whose main function was the orderly killing of millions of people? Even the early reports of the slaughter of thousands in the forests of Poland had seemed unreal. To simply imagine, much less to believe fully in the existence of a Majdanek, a Treblinka, an Auschwitz—this was a challenge to the mind far greater than the visualizing of World War I propaganda such as the "rape of Belgium."

If one looks closely at the problem, then, an explanation for the "double vision" of Bracker, Kirk, Gully, and the American public may really lie in a failure of imagination rather than in a simple analogy with discredited atrocity tales from 1914-18. It was not so much that Americans balked at full belief because of a propaganda legacy, but rather because the stories themselves seemed beyond the realm of what they could imagine. This phenomenon has been noticed by Walter Laqueur, who also found that disbelief existed side-by-side with knowledge when it came to reports of Nazi genocide. He told the story of Jan Karski, an extraordinarily daring Pole who in 1942 first smuggled himself into and then escaped from the Belzec death camp. Late in that year Karski embarked on a mission to the capitals of the West, telling his story to all who would listen and urging action against the slaughter. In Washington he met, among others, Supreme Court Justice Felix Frankfurter. Frankfurter stood horrified at Karski's revelations, but told him that he could not believe him. Karski protested, and Frankfurter clarified his statement. He had no doubt, he said, that Karski was telling the truth. He simply could not believe him.[10]

The problem of imagining Nazi genocide becomes even clearer if one looks at the outer limits of description presented to the American public by fervently anti-Nazi writers and filmmakers during the war. For these makers of culture, the double vision involved an abstract acceptance of what had been reported but, as it turned out, an extraordinarily limited ability to conceive the magnitude and detail of the horror. Stated simply, books published and motion pictures exhibited during the war envisioned a terrifying but sadly outdated sense of life under the Hitler regime. For example, in late 1943 Simon and Schuster published a widely reviewed and read collection entitled *The Ten Commandments: Ten Short Novels of Hitler's War Against the Moral Code.* The list of authors was impressive: Thomas Mann, Rebecca West, Franz Werfel, John Erskine, Bruno Frank, Jules Romains, André Maurois, Sigrid Undset, Hendrik Willem van Loon, and Louis Bromfield. Each author created a story that illustrated the Nazis' transgressions of a particular commandment.[11]

The novellas themselves, aside from an opening piece by Thomas Mann that retold Moses' sojourn on Mount Sinai, recounted sometimes melodramatic confrontations of human decency with Nazi rule. In one story a half-Jewish opera star is forced to claim that she was born of an affair her mother had with an

Aryan man. The lie destroyed father, mother, and daughter. In another, a German soldier finds himself pushed by the logic of his position to murder his beloved old French professor, who once had taught in Germany but who had become a thorn in the side of the German occupation in France. Only in Rebecca West's "Thou Shalt Not Make Any Graven Image" does there appear a scene that even begins to hint at the worst situations. Two brave Scandinavian playwrights and the non-Jewish wife of a deported Jewish writer defy the Nazi occupation to the point of being deported themselves. The final scenes take place as the three resisters are put with Jews in a sealed freight car heading for Poland. It is the closest image in wartime popular fiction to the reality of the transports.[12]

As for the camps, the public's familiarity with concentration camp life came from one major source, Anne Seghers's novel *The Seventh Cross*. A vivid story of resistance and escape from a camp in prewar Germany, it was later made into a gripping and popular movie starring Spencer Tracy, Signe Hasso, and Hume Cronyn. It included accounts of sadistic torture and death, but mainly dealt with themes of personal heroism and betrayal, and of the vindictiveness of the Nazi regime.[13] Of other movies that depicted Nazi cruelty, none was more vivid than Fritz Lang's *Hangmen Also Die,* released in 1943. It told of the assassination of Reinhard Heydrich, one of the architects of Nazi genocide, and the terror that followed in Czechoslovakia (including the demolition of the town of Lidice).

Whether in the case of *The Ten Commandments, The Seventh Cross, Hangmen Also Die,* or scores of works like them, the prevalent image was one of Nazi cruelty and sadism. But it was a cruelty usually aimed at political opposition. Innocents died, but in events set in motion by heroic defiance to Nazi rule. These works presented a readily recognizable logic for Nazi violence, one that allowed the comprehension of such events as the destruction of Lidice. It was, after all, a reprisal. Anne Seghers's concentration camp was an extremely cruel prison for political offenders (much like the original camps), again a recognizable and understandable entity. As such these and other works of popular culture became important molders of the public vision of the Nazis.

The very same works that offered a powerful indictment of the Germans, however, also set the imagination's limits in regard to Nazi terror. What could be worse than cruel political repression, or the destruction of an entire innocent village in retaliation for an assassination? The more sordid facts of mass slaughter, labor and death camps, Nazi policies of enslavement of peoples deemed inferior and extermination of Europe's Jews, though known through news sources and widely publicized since 1942, rarely found a place in portrayals of the enemy. While accepted in some rudimentary way as true, they seemed too extreme and unlikely to find a place in fiction.

Yet to brand the facts of genocide impossible to imagine only begs a deeper question: Why? It was certainly true that the artifacts of the camps—gas chambers, crematoria, massive warehouses to store booty from the dead—and the enormity of Nazi plans were new things under the sun, seemingly without precedent at least in scale and implementation. However, the facts themselves were perhaps not even the most effective bar to acceptance. It was rather what those facts signified to those who read them. And the awful truth was that they presented the possibility of death with no chance of escape, death without meaning or logic. As with war itself, death in the media versions of Nazi terror spoke to heroism, defiance, and it fortified the hope that a more positive human spirit would survive and emerge triumphant. But what of mass death, whether in the ditch at Babi Yar or in the gas chambers of Auschwitz? Here there was no promise but the end of life, stripped of its cultural meaning and reduced to an impersonal disappearance. There was no redeeming value and certainly no hope for the future.

Nor could one easily avoid a sense of complicity. Early on, in early 1942, Reinhold Niebuhr speculated as to why the liberal world in the West, Jews and non-Jews, did not spring instantly to the aid of European Jews or at least squarely face the fact of their peril. "We will not face it," he wrote, "because we should be overwhelmed by a sense of guilt in contemplating those aspects of the problem which Hitler did not create but only aggravated." He was painfully aware that the place of Jews in American life, for instance, remained a hotly debated public issue, and that the Nazi solution grew out of extensions of a similar debate in Germany. Nor, he argued, could even the Jews fully face the basic implication of such common roots, for then they might have to "recognize that the solutions provided by the liberal Jewish world [assimilation or toleration] have failed to reach the depths of the problem." Niebuhr did not mention the state of blacks in America, affected by racial laws in many ways quite similar to those restricting Jews in prewar Germany, although it would have only strengthened his argument.[14]

Niebuhr showed great insight. The Nazis could not be written off as products of some primitive culture, he asserted, for they had grown up in one of the most advanced societies in Europe, and shared with Americans and the rest of the West racial, religious, and ethnic attitudes that were the precondition for Auschwitz. In many ways they were us, and that was difficult to face.

It is hard to know whether some more direct envisioning of Nazi terror, if possible, would have moved Americans and others in the West to greater action to save Europe's Jews and the millions of others enslaved in the camps. Certainly enough was known and comprehended to make a case for action, and thousands of American Jews and Christians urged their government to make special efforts to save those in peril. Going beyond mere appeal, they raised hundreds of thousands of dollars to help those who could escape. At the same time, knowing the same facts, the Roosevelt administration and Churchill's government in England moved slowly if at all. They argued that the best way to save those enslaved by the Nazis was to win the war, an argument that was certainly correct. It was one that also neatly sidestepped such issues as the possibility of Allied sponsored secret rescue operations, changes in domestic immigration laws to allow for refugees, and, in the case of the British, more liberal access to Palestine for Jews.

It is debatable whether more direct proof of Nazi atrocities would have shocked Britain and America into action. What is not debatable is the simple fact that few in the West, no matter their knowledge of Nazi genocide or their commitment to Europe's Jews, were quite prepared for the scenes revealed that spring of

1945. Unlike Natzwiller, the camps later overrun by American and British units had not been abandoned. Indeed, they had become the dumping grounds for survivors of the Nazi experiment in slave labor and genocide. The liberations made horrified believers out of the skeptics and brought a new and hideous sense of reality even to those who never doubted the worst. The novelist Meyer Levin, during the war a correspondent whose special personal mission had been to aid Jewish refugees, wrote of his visit to Ohrdruf, the first of the camps to be uncovered by American armies: "We had known. The world had vaguely heard. But until now no one of us had looked on this. Even this morning we had not imagined we would look on this. It was as though we had penetrated at last to the center of the black heart, to the very crawling inside of the vicious heart."[15]

2 | Ohrdruf and Nordhausen

On April 4, 1945, Meyer Levin was traveling with the Fourth Armored Division as it moved through Gotha in its inexorable drive east. He had a traveling companion, Erik, an escaped prisoner of war and French Jew who was now searching for his mother, who had been sent to a concentration camp. Levin and his companion came upon some "cadaverous refugees" along the road. "They were like none we had ever seen," Levin later wrote: "skeletal, with feverish sunken eyes, shaven skulls." They identified themselves as Poles and beckoned the two strangers toward the site where they had been held prisoner. The Germans were gone, they assured them. The Poles' broken German began to make more and more sense as they talked about "people buried in a big hole" and "Death commando." It was clear they were describing a camp, but the road was too dark and potentially dangerous. They waited for light.[1]

The next morning one of the Poles took them to Ohrdruf, named for and just outside a small town due south of Gotha. They drove through the gate and immediately confronted a pile of dead prisoners, all in striped uniforms. The corpses were fleshless, and at the back of each skull was a bullethole. The Pole then took them to a shed that held a stack of stiff and naked men. "The bodies were flat and yellow as lumber," he remembered. ". . . Erik uttered not a word. So it was like this. So his mother had been in a place like this."

Bodies near main gate, Ohrdruf, April 8, 1945.

Ohrdruf had actually been discovered by accident. On April 4 and 5 of 1945, units of the Fourth Armored Division of the Third Army moved on Gotha and Ohrdruf, just west of Weimar along the Autobahn, in search of a secret Nazi communications center. The towns were taken without much struggle and part of the communications center was located.[2] Scouts reconnoitering the surrounding country found the camp and came back with the message, according to veteran Joseph Kushlis, that just over the crest of the hill was a sight one would not believe even when one saw it. On the way into the camp at Ohrdruf, Kushlis noticed two men sitting on a barracks stoop, with eyes that appeared to be "nothing but dark holes in their skull and face." At least they were alive, for the panorama the Americans came upon was what Levin had seen—the dead scattered on the open grounds between barracks, as individuals or in piles, and in heaps hidden inside the barracks. One corpse seemed fresher than the others. After photographing it, Kushlis found out why. This very man had greeted the first American soldiers in the camp and offered to show them around. As he gave his tour a Polish prisoner came up to him and, in full sight of the Americans, hit him with a piece of lumber and stabbed him to death. The dead man had been a guard parading as a prisoner.[3]

I guess the most vivid recollection of the whole camp is the pyre that was located on the edge of the camp. It was a big pit, where they had stacked bodies, stacked bodies and wood and burned them. I guess I'll never forget the ashes, it looked like there was a whole hip burning, and I touched it with a stick, and it just fell apart. —Frank Hamburger, an infantryman who saw Ohrdruf[4]

Bodies in shed, Ohrdruf, April 12, 1945.

Pyre of bodies found at Ohrdruf, April 13, 1945.

Survivor of Ohrdruf.

(*Witness to the Holocaust*)

Ohrdruf had been a labor camp, its inmates forced to dig vast caverns that housed underground headquarters and transportation. As many as 10,000 men had lived and slaved at Ohrdruf; very few survived. In its last days, with the arrival of the Americans imminent, the SS had either marched most of the prisoners to other camps or killed them. Small in comparison to other camps, without the sophisticated equipment of death and torture found elsewhere, it was in fact a minor sub-camp of Buchenwald. Yet its significance lay in the fact that it was the first remains of a camp to be discovered by either the British or American armies that actually contained prisoners and corpses, and as such was a revelation.

On April 12, Generals George Patton, Omar Bradley, and Dwight Eisenhower toured the camp at the invitation of the XX Corps commander, in whose zone Ohrdruf fell. The generals had begun the day in a jovial mood, and why not? Their armies had advanced into the heart of central Germany and had begun to prepare for the final campaign of the war. They were making routine visits to Corps headquarters, and spent the morning with XII Corps near Merkers. There they were shown a mine in which lay a part of the German gold reserve and much more. As the mine elevator descended on its one thin cable, Patton glanced at the army brass present and quipped that promotions would be stimulated if the cable didn't hold. "O.K., George, that's enough," came Ike's voice from the dark. "No more cracks until we are above ground again." At the bottom and a short tunnel away the entourage came upon a large room of crates, paper money, gold coin and bullion, jewelry, paintings, gold and silver fillings and bridgework—perhaps over a hundred million dollars in booty strewn and stacked, a symbolic storehouse of the Nazi plunder of Europe's peoples and cultures.[5]

After lunch the generals moved on to XX Corps headquarters at Gotha, whose commander had specially requested a visit in order to show his superiors a less glittering site—the concentration camp at Ohrdruf. The generals, though used to carnage in many forms, were shocked. "The smell of death overwhelmed us even before we passed through the stockade," Bradley remembered five years later. "More than 3,200 naked, emaciated bodies had been flung into shallow graves. Others lay in the streets where they had fallen. Lice crawled over the yellowed skin of their sharp, bony frames." Bradley recalled that Eisenhower turned pale and silent, but insisted on seeing the whole camp. And that they saw, from the shed piled to the ceiling with bodies, to various torture devices, to a butcher's block used for smashing gold fillings from the mouths of the dead (some of which no doubt had ended up in the Merkers mine). Patton retired behind a barracks and became physically ill.[6]

Eisenhower, Bradley, and Patton view pyre at Ohrdruf, April 12, 1945.

Eisenhower seethed with a silent anger that he vented on a hapless G.I. as the group waited to leave. The young soldier had accidentally bumped into a Nazi ex-guard and let loose a nervous giggle. "General Eisenhower fixed him with a cold eye," Patton's aide Charles Codman wrote his wife, "and when he spoke, each word was like the drop off an icicle. 'Still having trouble hating them?' he said." Later still, a day that began with a quip in the Merkers mine only to move to the incredible scene at Ohrdruf, ended with the news that Roosevelt had died.

Soon after seeing Ohrdruf, Eisenhower ordered every unit near by that was not in the front lines to tour Ohrdruf: "We are told that the American soldier does not know what he is fighting for. Now, at least, he will know what he is fighting *against*."[7] Eisenhower felt it was essential not only for his troops to see for themselves, but for the world to know about conditions at Ohrdruf and other camps. From Third Army headquarters he cabled London and Washington, urging delegations of officials and newsmen to be eye-witnesses to the camps. The message to Washington read: "We are constantly finding German camps in which they have placed political prisoners where unspeakable conditions exist. From my own personal observation, I can state unequivocally that all written statements up to now do not paint the full horrors."[8]

Even as the small hell of Ohrdruf was registering in the minds of the commanding officers, other U.S. Army units were uncovering new and more awful conditions due north of Ohrdruf, near the town of Nordhausen. The Nordhausen-Dora complex of labor camps had been built in 1943 to supply labor for building V-2 factories in man-made caves dug out of the Harz Mountains. The initial prisoner population of twelve thousand actually lived in the cold, damp tunnels as they built them; by late 1944 the Nazis had constructed flimsy barracks and a crematorium—the death rate was so high that it became impractical to ship the corpses back to Buchenwald, some fifty kilometers away, for cremation. This camp the Germans called Dora. Another location, closer to the town of Nordhausen itself, became a human dumping ground for Dora laborers who had grown too weary or sick for a full day's work. At Nordhausen (called the Boelke Kaserne by the Germans), prisoners festered with little food and reduced, but difficult, labor details. Anywhere from forty to seventy-five prisoners died per day, this in a population of four thousand.[9]

Units of the Third Army had overrun parts of Dora as early as April 6, but it was not until April 11 that the Timberwolf Division pulled into Nordhausen. It came upon 3000 corpses and more than seven hundred barely surviving inmates. The vast majority of both the living and the dead lay in two double-decker barracks, piled three to a bunk or half-hidden in mounds of excelsior and straw on the floor. Many were too weak to move, and the rooms reeked of death and excrement. Already prey to starvation and tuberculosis, the prisoners had also suffered numerous casualties from American bombings of the V-2 factories the week before. "Only a handful could stand on rickety, pipestem legs," wrote a *Newsweek* reporter on the scene. ". . . Their eyes were sunk deeply into their skulls and their skins under thick dirt were a ghastly yellow. Some sobbed great dry sobs to see the Americans. Others merely wailed pitifully, and one poor semiconscious Jew . . . kept crying 'Ey yaah'."[10] Colonel D. B. Hardin of the VIII Corps Military Government, whose job it was to evacuate survivors and otherwise put the camp in order after the liberation, told of pulling a survivor from between two corpses. "The man could speak," Hardin noted, "and that was about all." The case was not unusual.[11]

> Oh the odors, well there is no way to describe the odors. . . . Many of the boys I am talking about now—these were tough soldiers, there were combat men who had been all the way through on the invasion—were ill and vomiting, throwing up, just the sight of this. . . . —C. W. Doughty, 49th Engineers, Combat Battalion, attached to Third Armored Division at the time of the Nordhausen liberation[12]

Two liberated prisoners, Nordhausen, April 14, 1945.

[The prisoners] were so thin they didn't have anything—didn't have any buttocks to lie on; there wasn't any flesh on their arms to rest their skulls on . . . one man that I saw there who had died on his knees with his arms and head in a praying position and he was still there, apparently had been for days. —William B. Lovelady, commander of the task force of the Third Armored Division which captured Nordhausen[13]

I must also say that my fellow G.I.'s, most of them American born, had no particular feeling for fighting the Germans. They also thought that any stories they had read in the paper, or that I had told them out of first-hand experience, were either not true or at least exaggerated. And it did not sink in, what this was all about, until we got into Nordhausen. —Fred Bohm, an Austrian-born American soldier who helped liberate Nordhausen[14]

The Americans evacuated survivors to army hospitals or evicted Germans from apartments in town and used these living quarters as makeshift clinics. The dead, thousands of them, posed a greater challenge. First the bodies were taken from the barracks and laid side by side over an area of two acres. Two thousand townspeople, who had been forcibly enlisted for the burial effort, were divided into two groups. The first dug a series of trench graves 150 feet long and 5 feet wide, room enough for somewhere between fifty and a hundred bodies, on a hill overlooking the camp. The other group carried the corpses the half-mile between the camp and the burial trenches, sometimes two or four men to a body, in a seemingly endless procession.

We laboriously tried to pick out the ones who still showed signs of life. And we used the German civilians to help us in that; and, frankly, I must say that they were as sick as our guys were. . . . They always said that they had no idea that these things were going on, and in many instances it is possibly true, because certainly they weren't publicized. . . . And some of them refused to lend a hand because they said, "We had no part in this." And of course at that time, nobody would accept that as an excuse, and then they offered to pitch in. —Fred Bohm[15]

Civilians dig mass graves at Nordhausen, April 14, 1945.

German civilians carrying bodies to graves, Nordhausen, April 13, 1945.

Nordhausen dead in open graves awaiting burial, April 13, 1945.

We started getting these bodies and we wound up—I was told—the total number was about 2000, and we just had them in big long lines and I know our chaplain was just running up and down the lines, just straining and cursing and everything. . . . It was just a silent stink putrid death is. . . . I mean, you know, we would even communicate with each other in whispers and things like that, I don't know why you do that, don't ask me, you just do. . . . I guess half my thoughts were really prayers, but right at that point, we were trying to get these bodies out. We were afraid of disease and this kind of thing, and we wanted to get them under the ground and restore some sort of dignity to them, but then we had another mission after that one. . . . I guess really later the profoundness of the situation gradually came to me. —C. W. Doughty[16]

Surrounded at Nordhausen by masses of dead and dying and grotesque burials, the liberators experienced a partial numbing of emotion and physical sense that has been aptly labeled "psychic closing-off." Remembering the experience at Nordhausen with more than a touch of sad irony, C. W. Doughty put it another way: "It's just so wonderful that you can't fully grasp everything that you could see, otherwise you might not have endured."[17] These soldiers found themselves capable of confronting the awful tasks of sorting the living from the dead, breathing the fetid air, and walking amidst untold human misery only by partially shutting off their senses and emotions. They also distanced themselves from the scene around them by making a basic distinction between themselves and the dead or liberated. If the liberator defined the helpless victims of Nazis as not quite human, then he could defend himself against thinking that this might have been his own fate. Such a strategy, a part of the liberator experience at every camp, was illustrated in Al Newman's Nordhausen report that appeared in *Newsweek*. He captioned one part of the story "These Were Men" and later characterized the liberated prisoners as "creatures—you could not by any stretch of the imagination call them human beings." It was Newman's way of describing in the most graphic way possible the destruction that had been wrought in the lives of the

Nazis' victims. At the same time, by making these individuals something other than human, he could push from his mind the realization that anyone could be brutalized into such a state, that one's normal existence and even life was so fragile.[18]

Often, though, the defenses were not effective, and for a variety of reasons a strange and disturbing mixture of emotions surfaced and haunted the soul. This happened in the case of Morris Parloff, an intelligence officer who came to Nordhausen several days after the liberation in order to investigate the V-2 rocket factory tunnels at the camp. As a Jew, he was anxious to see European Jews, to help rescue them, to feel somehow at one with them. This somewhat romantic sense of identity had already been sobered some weeks before, when in an occupied German city he had come across a Jew who offered him aid. He thought it strange that there would be such a survivor in the city, one who seemed to have made it through the war with little problem. Soon he found out that the Jew had been a "finger man" for the Gestapo, roaming the city in search of remaining Jews. For Parloff it was a shock to see what a person might do to survive. He thought to himself: "How would I have done? Would I have had the courage to do otherwise? There was no way you could pass judgment."[19]

Nordhausen brought new and stranger experiences for Parloff. He got to the camp after the dead had been buried and most of the survivors had been taken to better quarters. In fact, he had expected to see an empty camp and to do his work in the rocket tunnels. Nothing had numbed his emotions, nothing had prepared him to repress the feelings that welled up when he found 120 Jews still in the tunnel and listened to their story. They had boarded the evacuation train like the rest, but were quickly thrown off by anti-Semitic fellow prisoners. Parloff found himself getting angry at the Jews themselves for allowing this to happen. As a Jew he felt shamed by them. Later, while taking a tour of the camp conducted by one of the Jewish prisoners, he had a more chilling experience. At one point, as Parloff stood in dazed silence before the crematorium, his guide climbed up and stood upon a pile of white ashes near by. "You know what I'm standing on?" he asked him matter of factly, and began to answer, "I'm standing on the bodies of . . . ." "I

Two liberated slave laborers and a V-2 rocket tail, Nordhausen, April 12, 1945.

screamed at him to get off," Parloff remembered, "and he looked at me very puzzled like what kind of morality is that? I realized I didn't understand him, and he didn't understand me, and there was a great barrier between us. . . . I really felt alien, more than alien, it was through a wish that I wasn't fully aware of to disassociate myself: That is different . . . those people are different . . . I don't belong there."[20]

Nonetheless Lieutenant Parloff felt it imperative to get the Jews to better quarters, and took time out from his V-2 inspections to arrange a special train to take them out of Nordhausen to a recovery area. An army major with whom he was dealing in this matter made a snide remark about doing something special to aid his "co-religionists," implying that such treatment was somehow unethical. Caught between his own uneasy feelings and the wisecrack of a non-Jew, Parloff snapped back into his sense of

Survivors of Nordhausen, April 1945. *(Witness to the Holocaust)*

Nordhausen, April 1945. *(Witness to the Holocaust)*

identity with the survivors. And later, when German civilians complained of marauding bands of freed Jews, he sought the renegades out just to talk with them and to come into contact with Jews who were defiant.

Parloff had discovered a truth most others would experience if not fully understand. The world of the camps was a perverse universe unto itself, where death had become as common as breathing, and the dead a collective pile of dust. He had confronted something in himself and had experienced the perversion of human dignity that anti-Semitism had wrought in and out of the camps. The gulf of experience and expectation that lay between liberator and survivor, the different world that made battle-weary Americans innocents by comparison, disoriented and disturbed even those most ready to embrace the victims of Nazi terror. An almost unbearable mixture of empathy, disgust, guilt, anger, and alienation pervaded each entry into a camp, compounding the palpable horror that greeted the liberator in each barracks and on every parade ground.

3 | Buchenwald

It is said that often Goethe would leave his Weimar residence and, on a fine spring or summer day, ascend into the beech forest north of the city to commune with nature and write poetry. One spring day Percy Knauth took off on his motorcycle and headed up a hilly road to the same woods, but for a different reason. It was 1938, and Knauth was a young American reporter investigating rumors of torture, exhausting physical labor, and the breaking of minds and wills—all at a new prison camp named Buchenwald. Those who had been released from Buchenwald were too fearful to confirm the stories, and the camp's SS officers who wandered down to Weimar for women and wine didn't talk about their work. Nonetheless within a year of its opening in 1937, Buchenwald had become a lurid legend to rival Dachau. So Knauth thought he would nose around the perimeter of the camp. He kept his distance in this "forbidden" territory, always fearful that a guard might stop him or, worse still, that a bullet might prevent him from delivering the lame excuse that he had somehow gotten lost. He managed to see an occasional stretch of barbed-wire and the silhouette of a distant watchtower, and once he peered down into a deep quarry at the edge of the forest, on whose far side he saw a small crowd of prisoners in striped uniforms. That was all.

Seven years and a war later, Knauth returned, this time to report on the camp's liberation. "Buchenwald is beyond all comprehension," he observed on that occasion. "You just can't understand it, even when you've seen it."[1]

45

Much had changed between 1938 and 1945. The Nazis built Buchenwald as a camp for political prisoners (mostly German Communists and Social Democrats), certain classes of incorrigible criminals, and—as the government stepped up its anti-Semitic campaign in 1937-38—for Jews. The site they chose had as its centerpiece the so-called Goethe oak, a tree stump that marked the poet's favorite spot in the woods. This stroke of Nazi black humor had behind it a more sinister purpose: the hidden, forbidding woods so close to Weimar provided a perfect setting for a camp that must remain a mystery yet be ever present in the minds of those who contemplated opposition to the regime.

Whatever Buchenwald's gruesome reputation before the war, the gross butchery of Nazi death squads in Poland and Russia and, by 1941, the creation of the Polish extermination camps put a new light on Buchenwald's torture and slow death. It acquired the reputation of being a "mild" camp. Its population leveled off at more or less 15,000, and the SS somewhat routinized life at Buchenwald through the use of a network of prison trustees. At first this invisible government was dominated by the "greens," non-political and often sadistic criminals whose prison garb sported a green triangle. There resulted a fearful and violent order in the camp, one that made death from overwork and malnutrition (not to mention violent punishment and medical experiments) commonplace. Still the camp's primary purpose was not systematic extermination. That constituted the meaning of mild.

This relatively stable system began to disintegrate in 1942 and continued to do so through to the end of the war. The basic pressure was population. Buchenwald became a center for supply of slave labor in war industries, and filled its labor pool with prisoners from France and Belgium and ever-increasing shipments of evacuees from the death and labor camps in the East. The perimeters of the old camp became tent cities to hold new arrivals; subcamps began to extend out into the Harz Mountains; and health and sanitary conditions for most prisoners deteriorated from their already minimal levels. Especially awful was the new "Little Camp," a section of crude barracks earmarked for Jews, Gypsies, and those sick and exhausted prisoners from the main camp who had outlived their usefulness.

At the same time, there had been a veritable revolution in the governance of the camp. Karl Koch had been Buchenwald's first commandant. From the beginning he had sought ways of filling his own pockets by selling the property taken from camp prisoners and by running a black market in food and material meant for the camp. Such behavior ran counter to the SS ideal of orderly corporate plunder, but Koch bribed a sufficient number of his fellow officers to avoid prosecution. However, local Thuringian officials made enough complaints about the commandant's nonpayment of taxes to force the SS to transfer Koch to Majdanek in 1942. He so ill-managed that camp that he was tried and convicted by an SS court and executed for his crimes.[2]

Meanwhile, in all this upheaval, the new commandant Hermann Pister allowed a German Communist prisoner group, some of them original inmates of the camp, to wrest power from the "greens." The Communist prisoners reduced the amount of black marketeering and other common corruption, cut down the amount of wanton sadism on the part of prisoner trustees (or Kapos), and made plans for the ultimate takeover of the camp in case of Nazi defeat. But in other ways the Communists merely shifted the ground of corruption to the assignment of work details, food, medical care, and ultimately life. From their takeover until the end of the war, favored treatment was often received on the basis of political loyalties. The Nazis, for their part, gained from the Communist regime a more predictable work force and a greater sense of order.

By 1945 the camp had grown to a population approaching fifty thousand and had become, by its own standards at least, a society of extremes: a relatively favored group of German Communist, German, and Western European prisoners at the top; Jews, Gypsies, Eastern Europeans, and other disfavored elements in the "Little Camp" at the bottom. This social division literally took on topographic form. The original camp sat above the "Little Camp," with a barbed-wire gate to separate them.

American advances put new pressure on the camp in late March and early April 1945, and a strange drama began to be enacted with Commandant Pister at the center. Berlin had ordered Pister to evacuate, kill, or otherwise get rid of the prisoner population. Pister was of two minds about the order. He was no humanitarian and normally followed orders, but he saw the handwriting on the wall and hoped to present himself to the Americans as a relatively benign presence. To follow Himmler's drastic orders would hardly help support such an image. One of the various underground prisoner organizations, playing on this pragmatic side of Pister, forged a communiqué from the American forces that promised leniency if he handed over the camp and its population in good shape. Meanwhile the Communist underground, having more direct control of the everyday life of the camp, planned ways of resisting the evacuation orders.[3]

Pister attempted to steer a middle course. Between April 3 and April 10 more than 20,000 inmates, half of them Jews, were transported out of the camp. Most of them died on their way to Flossenburg, Dachau, and Theresienstadt. The transports might have claimed twice that number had the Communist-led prisoner committee and other groups not engaged in delaying tactics and outright refusal to follow orders. Pister, for his part, allowed the prisoners to resist without the usual terrible reprisals. Indeed, by April 10 Pister and most of the SS had fled, leaving a skeleton guard to resist the rapidly advancing Americans.[4]

Communist prisoners and Allied underground groups had, over the preceding year, built up a small cache of arms stolen from the SS or painstakingly built from parts smuggled by prisoners working in the nearby armaments plant. They readied themselves for revolt. On the morning of April 11 the prisoners could already hear small-arms fire in the vicinity of the camp, and at one in the afternoon the lead tanks of the Fourth Armored Division could be seen from the heights of the camp. There is much controversy as to what happened next. Communist tradition has it that, with SS guards still in the towers, the prisoners arose, overpowered the Nazis and liberated themselves. Other accounts emphasize that by the afternoon most of the SS were gone; it was at that point, they say, that the prisoner rebels revealed their arms and paraded them with no real enemy in sight. In other words, they rose up in arms when there was no one to shoot and with only the possible motive of taking control of the camp before the Americans arrived. Which, in either case, is what they did.[5]

The first Americans at Buchenwald, in fact, came upon it by accident. At about noon on April 11, Combat Team 9 of the 9th Armored Infantry Battalion, Sixth Armored Division, took the nearby town of Hottelstedt. There they captured fifteen SS troops and lined them up to be sent to the rear. Suddenly about fifty Russian prisoners emerged from the woods and attempted to seize the SS. They were ordered to desist, did so, but pointed out that these Germans had been guards at Buchenwald concentration camp, just to the south and east. Going to Buchenwald would have been a detour for the Combat Team, whose mission was to drive east toward Ettersberg, but Captain Robert Bennett did send four of his men with some Russians as their guide to investigate the camp. They arrived about an hour after the "revolt" had occurred. Entering through a hole cut in the fence into the main upper camp, the prisoners cheered joyfully and hoisted one of the Americans, Captain Frederic Keffer, on their shoulders, tossed him in the air repeatedly, and only stopped when a somewhat jarred Keffer asked them to put him down. Keffer and his men distributed what rations and cigarettes they had and notified headquarters about the existence and location of the camp. They then left, having seen only the better part of the camp and a hint of what was to come—the prisoners had already pinned some of the captured SS to the ground with stakes.[6]

When, later in the day and in the ensuing week, members of the Fourth Armored Division and 80th Infantry took over administration and rehabilitation at Buchenwald, they began to comprehend that, unlike at Ohrdruf and Nordhausen, they had entered a complete if macabre society. The Americans were met by reasonably healthy looking, armed prisoners ready to help administer distribution of food, clothing, and medical care. These same prisoners, an International Committee with the Communist underground leader Hans Eiden at its head, seemed to have perfect disciplinary control over their fellow inmates. The prison committee saw as its primary mission the aiding and ordering of relief efforts. Their second and more visible goal was to deal summary justice to as many SS as they could locate. Survivors hunted the woods for escaped SS and searched among the liberated prisoners themselves for Nazis who had traded their uniforms for concentra-

The gate at Buchenwald, April 1945.

A welcome slogan in the Main Camp, Buchenwald, April 1945.

tion camp stripes. In all, liberated prisoners killed almost eighty ex-guards and camp functionaries in the days following the liberation, sometimes with the aid and encouragement of Americans.

> [It] almost killed me: one of the inmates of the camp when we got up close to two Nazi SS types, kicked the corpse. And that just expressed hatred more vividly than anything you could possibly imagine. —Kenneth Bowers, 19th Tactical Air Command[7]

> Fred Mercer of XX Corps remembered one instance where a German soldier attempted to surrender to the Americans, but was intercepted by a prisoner with a four-foot wood log: "He just stood there and beat him to death. He had to—of course, we didn't bother him."[8]

Of course all around these displays of rage and revenge lay Buchenwald's vast fields of human misery and death. Even in the upper camp there was the crematorium with its half-burned bodies still in place; piles of corpses left unburned because the coal supply ran out; and the emaciated survivors of that part of the camp known for its relatively good treatment. Despite the first impression made by the International Committee and those prisoners who were healthy enough to seek revenge, it soon became apparent that liberated Buchenwald was also a village of aching and bewildered human beings.

My first impression of it was the odor. The stench of it was all over the place and there were a bunch of very bewildered, lost individuals who came to me pathetically at the door in their unkempt uniforms to see what we were doing and what was going to be done about them. They were staying at the camp even though their guards and staff had fled because they didn't know where to go or what to do. They had heard news that the Americans had taken over that area and they were waiting for somebody to turn their lives back straight again and they were just lost souls at that time.

Well, my feeling was that this was the most shattering experience of my life. —John Glustrom, 333rd Engineers[9]

Main Camp, Buchenwald, April 1945.   (*Witness to the Holocaust*)

Buchenwald, April 1945.

Then there was the Little Camp. At liberation its population was made up of Jews, Gypsies, worn-out laborers, and evacuees from other camps. Most of the 700 children at Buchenwald were in the Little Camp, including a three-year-old child. Both prisoners and barracks offered a somber contrast to the big camp. As opposed to the solid buildings of the main compound, the structures in the Little Camp were dismal barns, each with three to five tiers of wide shelves running the length of the building. On some of the shelves were rudimentary mattresses of rotting straw, covered with vermin. In the center, between the barracks ran an open concrete ditch that gave off an indescribably horrible stench—it was the sole latrine.

The buildings only hinted at the condition of the prisoners.

Barracks meant for 450 housed 1000 to 1200 inhabitants. The shelves were stacked with the living, the near dead, and in some cases the truly dead. Even after liberation, every day twenty to twenty-five prisoners in each Little Camp block died.

These prisoners were held in such contempt by both the Nazis and the prisoner leadership of the main camp that even days after the liberation the barbed wire gate to the compound was still locked, and the most sadistic of the Kapos still ruled in each barracks. When on April 12 a massive ceremony of freedom was held on the main square of the camp, the prisoners of the Little Camp rotted in their barracks.

Soon after the liberation of Buchenwald two American psychological warfare observers, a civilian Egon Fleck and 1st Lieutenant Edward A. Tenenbaum, entered the *Kleines Lager* as part of their extensive survey of conditions at Buchenwald. "Even now," they wrote in a secret report, "a trip through the Little Camp is like a nightmare":

Survivors at Buchenwald, April 1945.

On the sight of an American uniform a horde of gnomes and trolls seems to appear like magic, pouring out of doorways as if shot from a cannon. Some hop on crutches. Some hobble on stumps of feet. Some run with angular movements. Some glide like Oriental genies. Almost all wear striped convict suits, covered with patches, or grey-black remnants of Eastern clothing. The universal covering is a little black skull cap. They doff these ceremoniously to the visitors. Some are crying, others shouting with joy.[10]

Percy Knauth made sure to see the Little Camp. He was accompanied by a Czech surgeon who had been a prisoner at the time of liberation, and who continued to live among his fellow survivors and aid them as he could. Knauth peered into the surgeon's own dark barracks, and was told that 1500 men lived inside. "It was a long, dim room full of murmurs and movements of figures in all kinds of clothes," Knauth wrote, "from the striped uniform to just a sack draped over bony shoulders."

As Knauth's eyes became accustomed to the darkness, he could see a rag-tag tangle of men "emaciated beyond all imagination or description." Their legs and arms were sticks with "huge bulging joints," and their loins were fouled by their own excrement. "Their eyes were sunk so deep that they looked blind," he remembered. "If they moved at all, it was with a crawling slowness that made them look like huge, lethargic spiders. Many just lay in their bunks as if dead."[11] Knauth, in response to a request for food, pulled a chocolate bar out of his pocket. "The spidery men in the dimness galvanized into sudden motion," he wrote. "A dozen hands reached for the chocolate bar, clutching wildly. The filthy bodies pressed around me, pushed me, nearly knocked me down. I fought for sanity and kept repeating: *'Moment, moment!'*" One man finally reached the chocolate, but no sooner had he grasped it than others pounced on him. "I saw the chocolate in several filthy hands, brown melted gobs of it," Knauth remembered. "—then it was gone."[12]

Like the Americans at Nordhausen, Knauth and others soon found they could function only by repressing all emotion, however unwillingly. "Numbly, I saw death now," Knauth wrote of his

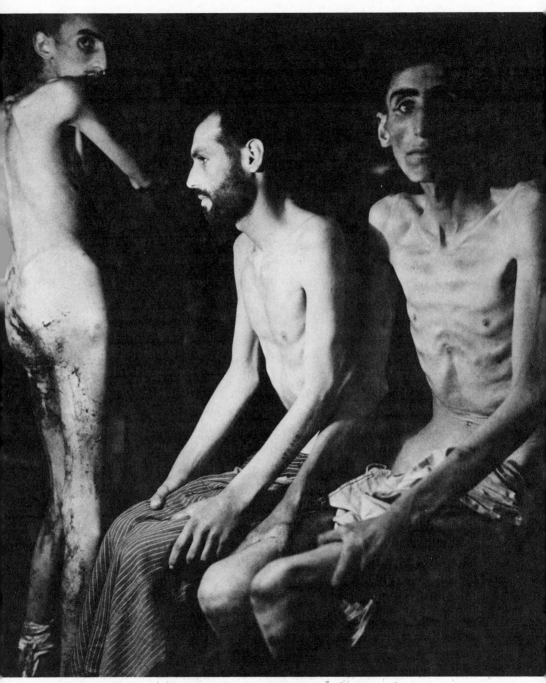

Survivors of Buchenwald's "Little Camp," April 16, 1945.

Buchenwald visit, "and before I left the camp that evening I saw it reduced to such ordinariness that it left me feeling nothing, not even sickness at my stomach."[13] For Margaret Bourke-White, whose stunning photographs of Buchenwald opened the eyes of the American public as few other individual photographers had been able to, the camera itself became her shield from the reality she was recording, from the "white horror" in front of her. "People often ask me how it is possible to photograph such atrocities," she later noted in her autobiography. "I have to work with a veil over my mind. In photographing the murder camps, the protective veil was so tightly drawn that I hardly knew what I had taken until I saw prints of my own photographs."[14]

There were dangers, however, in this natural defense against horror. In some cases Americans ignored the Little Camp prisoners in favor of the healthier ones, in part simply to get away from them. Fleck and Tenenbaum warned that this might be a problem. "They are brutalized, unpleasant to look on," they wrote of the worst cases. "It is easy to adopt the Nazi theory that they are subhuman, for many have in fact been deprived of their humanity. It would be easy to continue favoring the big camp in the distribution of food, as has been done in the past, and, more important for the wretches of the small camp, in the distribution of medicine."[15] Anonymous, emaciated, naked or in rags, speaking strange languages, and often displaying craven behavior, Little Camp prisoners could easily be both pitied and avoided. These worst cases became symbols of horror, the stuff of nightmares, but otherwise remained in danger-ous anonymity.

A few Americans did get to know even the worst-treated survivors better, and they began to comprehend the extraordinary saga that lay behind each bent and spare body. Meyer Levin, who knew Yiddish, visited Buchenwald in the days after the arrival of the Americans. He made it a point to record the stories of these seemingly timeless wrecks, tales of suffering in the death and labor camps and scenes of cruelty and massacre almost beyond belief. Virtually every story was punctuated by some variant of the same line: "I saw it. I saw it with my own eyes." One Polish Jew, Mordecai Stiegler, a writer, affected him more than most. Stiegler was thirty, had lived in Warsaw, and indeed had manned the barricades with the Polish home guard when the Nazis entered the city in 1939. No sooner had the Germans taken over, however, than the Poles identified him as a Jew to the invaders. He was arrested, tortured, and one Nazi officer cut swastikas on his cheeks and forehead with a razor blade. Levin noted that the scars were still clearly visible on his thin face.

Stiegler was drafted into forced labor around the city and then shipped in a boxcar to a labor camp. It was the first of a series of such camps, and in each place many died and few survived. His luck held out, after a fashion. Sometimes he escaped, but always he was recaptured. This was the way Stiegler spent 1940. Oddly enough, so unorganized were Nazi plans for the Jews at this point that at times he was released, went home, and then was conscripted for a new slave labor assignment. By 1941 the decision to exterminate European Jewry had hardened; the massacres, once sporadic, became more and more predictable. At one point Stiegler was selected to be killed, but in the midst of the bedlam accompanying the machine-gun fire and the screams of the dying, he ran to a group selected for labor.

In 1942 he escaped a death march in the Lublin area. He witnessed mass murders and incredible acts of sadism, but somehow survived. For sixteen months he worked in a munitions plant, but was evacuated at the approach of the Russians. He had managed to survive ten months at Buchenwald, even finding the energy to instruct in secret the children of the Little Camp in Yiddish and Hebrew. In addition, he held "literary evenings" for his fellow inmates, in which they shared poetry and history and literature.

Now Stiegler was free. To most who saw him he was just one of the animals, without history or future, part of the refuse of the Little Camp. For Meyer Levin, Mordecai Stiegler represented something else. "Slowly I was coming to understand," he commented with no little sense of awe," what was indestructible in the human world."[16]

4 | A Landscape of Terror

Although contemporary headlines and our own memories tend to focus on major camps like Buchenwald, these were hardly isolated institutions in an otherwise innocent German landscape. Every day American, British, and French soldiers encountered one remnant or another of a slave labor system that had become an important part of Germany's war economy. Through careful planning the SS had become an economic kingdom in its own right and seen to it that its slaves were exploited in just about every sector of German mining, agriculture, and industrial production. Literally millions of men and women from every Nazi-occupied nation as well as Jews and Gypsies slated for extinction fueled German productivity and made money for their SS overseers.

Each major camp was the center of a system of sub-camps, and sub-sub-camps even existed to supply labor for one or another industry. Hundreds of camps large and small dotted virtually every region in Germany, Austria, and occupied Poland. For instance, between 1933 and 1945 the Dachau administration controlled and supplied prisoners for a total of 240 auxiliary camps, each created to serve a particular construction project or factory. Some existed for only a month, others for years. Among the companies that dipped regularly into this slave labor pool were BMW, the auto manufacturer, as well as major civilian construction firms in the Munich area. In addition to labor camps there were also to be found, especially toward the end of the war, so-called transit camps to house evacuees on their way to a new labor assignment or to some form of annihilation.

From the beginning of their entry into Germany, American soldiers ran across these smaller camps and met slave laborers on the road. These less well-publicized camps never made a place for themselves in popular consciousness, but to those who saw them the shock of their uncovering and what they revealed about the importance and visibility of slave labor in Germany made no less an impression.

On May 2, General James Gavin's 82nd Airborne Division moved as far as Ludwigslust in northern Germany and accepted the surrender of 150,000 German soldiers, equipment and all. It was one more joyful portent of the end of the war. The next morning General Gavin received the news that the mayor of Ludwigslust and his wife had committed suicide. It seemed like an odd moment for such an act, but two days later Gavin knew why. In searching the outskirts of Ludwigslust, his personnel discovered Woebbelin. Unlike Buchenwald and Dachau, this camp had no long history, having been set up just months before as a transit camp for prisoners evacuated from areas threatened by the Allied advance in both the East and the West. Woebbelin had no internal prisoner structure, and anarchy reigned as a mixture of Poles, Hungarians, Russians, Jews, and Western Europeans competed for survival. With a shrinking food and water supply and a frightful increase in disease, death became an everyday occurrence and so did the battles among the prisoners themselves for the dwindling sustenance provided. In the last days some even turned to cannibalism. In the week the Americans came, one thousand died of starvation.[1]

A liberated inmate at Woebblin who thinks he will not be evacuated, May 4, 1945.

We walked inside and saw these skinny people who were still living, and one of my enlisted men who walked in with me realized they were starving and we had nothing but some candy bars, which we got in a ration, and one of my men gave the candy bar to one of these people who grabbed it and ran away and gulped it down so fast that he became unconscious and probably choked on it when he tried to swallow it before someone took it away from him. These Jewish people and these Polish people were like animals, they were so degraded, there was no goodness, no kindness, nothing of that nature, there was no sharing. If they got a piece of something to eat, they grabbed it and ran away in a corner and fought off anyone who came near them. —Samuel Glasshow, who helped liberate Woebbelin[2]

Survivor of Woebbelin being loaded on truck for transport to hospital.

Survivors of Woebbelin.

Those on the scene witnessed conditions as bad or worse than in the Little Camp at Buchenwald. The dead, the dying, human beings reduced to behavior many saw as animal-like, these were difficult things to face. Some dealt with these scenes by treating them as one had already learned to treat the battle deaths of enemies and strangers. "It was the same as coming upon where a mortar shell landed," remembered J. D. Digilio, "and you come across eight or ten German soldiers who have been killed. You know there was no sense of identification." Interestingly, it was only after learning about the fuller significance of the camps that Digilio saw his experience differently. However, at the time he recalled that his immediate concern was whether conditions at Woebbelin might be any indication of what was happening to American prisoners of war.[3]

For Samuel Glasshow, perhaps in part because as a Jew he could not think of the victims as simple strangers, the comparison with combat deaths came out differently. He had seen many people killed, even saw his commanding officer with his face blown off by a mortar shell. He'd treated hundreds of men, Americans and even some Germans. "I saw all kinds of gore and blood and intestines and whatnot," he noted. "I never saw anything like this [Woebbelin], because when I walked out of there, my feet were full of rotten feces, meat, garbage, and the smell was unbelievable."[4]

Indeed, Glasshow's experiences at Woebbelin encompassed extraordinary swings of engagement and revulsion. As a medical officer, he was able to help and did, but always with the deep and contradictory impulse to leave the camp. "This horror was of such a nature that I couldn't wait to get away . . . and get that smell out of my nose and wipe the dirt off my feet, and yet I went back . . . I don't know what I went back for, I don't know, maybe to get a souvenir or bring it back to have something tangible to think about . . . ." He also was deeply disturbed by the Germans. "They didn't admit responsibility," he recalled, "and the only sadness they showed, I think, was horror at what they saw. I think had they won the war, these people would have all been extermi-

Chaplain helps a liberated prisoner board an evacuation truck, Woebbelin, May 4, 1945.

nated, without any remorse on the civilians' part. I don't think they had any remorse. They were all brainwashed to the fact that these people were subhuman species."

Glasshow had one particularly telling experience with a German in Ludwigslust, who like many suggested that the Americans and Germans get together to destroy the Russians: "Then I said that, you know I am a Jew. We began to laugh; he said those Jews were the cause of this whole war—he didn't believe that I was Jewish and when I insisted on that he became terrified. He thought we would kill him."

In the end, however, it was among the conquered that Glasshow found relief. He was transferred to Berlin, and there he met "Germans who were healthy." In particular he became friends with a beautiful dental assistant: "I listened to her story. I was more interested in that than I was in thinking about this terrible decay and starvation."[5]

General Gavin was so outraged by what he saw at Woebbelin that he ordered all the people of Ludwigslust ten years of age and older to visit the camp. Then able-bodied civilians were required to rebury the dead and to create a permanent cemetery in the town. An individual grave was marked for each victim, about a quarter of them with Jewish stars and the rest with Christian crosses. The army chaplain conducted a combination Jewish, Protestant, and Catholic service.[6]

For many American soldiers, contact with the camps and slave labor system came in fleeting moments on the roads and in the towns of Germany. Along the way they encountered bands of displaced persons, small groups of dead and dying prisoners, and singular atrocities. These brushes with horror lived long in their minds. David Campbell, a company commander of the 180th Engineers, had several such experiences. His unit was attached to the Fifth Armored Division as it moved toward the Elbe north of Magdeburg. When Campbell's unit hit Braunschweig, sniper fire was encountered, and artillery fire was ordered in to help snuff out German resistance. The fire power blew off the doors of some

Service for dead of Woebbelin.

German POWs forced to view Woebbelin dead.

German civilians file past open graves for Woebbelin dead at Ludwigslust, May 7, 1945.

innocent-looking freight cars, which opened to reveal stacks of emaciated camp prisoners most of whom were dead. It seems that when American air strikes destroyed the train lines, the German guards attached to the shipment of prisoners (probably moving south to Dachau) simply shut the doors tight and left the area. Already starving and abandoned with no food and little air, the prisoners were doomed.[7]

As the Fifth Armored Division pressed east toward the Elbe, Campbell and his men came upon a different sort of scene at Fallersleben. Here, close to the city of Wolfsburg, the Germans had established a slave labor camp for a Volkswagen factory producing military vehicles. The day before the Americans arrived, the German guards fled leaving the workers to rampage through the camp and into town. The workers broke into the arsenal, raided the food stores, and more than a few died from wolfing down large quantities of raw flour. "Near there, there was a vermouth factory and they got into the vermouth," Campbell recalled. "Some of them were so drunk they'd stand on dikes or up on buildings and fire a gun and it'd knock 'em flat on their back." A number of the prisoners took tommy guns from the camp arsenal and marauded the countryside, setting fire to a number of houses and killing German civilians, including one mayor. A military government officer, whose job was to establish order, asked if Campbell and his men would help disarm the prisoners. It took all night.

After Fallersleben, Campbell was ordered northeast to Ousterburg, a town not far from the Elbe. On the way, he and his men noticed a large fire and much machine-gun and tank action. They investigated and found, near the town of Gardelegen, a sight more somber than that of drunken and rampaging liberated prisoners. They came upon the ruins of a barn, and the remains of hundreds of charred bodies. An SS unit transporting prisoners from the East had found itself caught in the American advance. Instead of surrendering, the SS herded the evacuees into the barn, poured gasoline over the structure and set it afire. Outside they waited with machine guns. Many prisoners were burned alive as they pressed on the doors; others lay in the open air, caught in

Scene of the Gardelegen atrocity.

German mayors view remains at Gardelegen, April 16, 1945.

Prisoner burned alive at Gardelegen, April 16, 1945.

SS machine-gun fire. Some were killed as they emerged from underneath the side walls, having dug themselves out of the burning barn. When American troops came on the scene, the first thing they noticed were the heads of these dead prisoners peering from underneath the wall. Close to forty years later the memory of it still bothered Campbell: "That kind of stuff you never get used to."[8]

Men of the First Army were shown a similar atrocity as they surged eastward toward the Elbe. On April 18th, as the fight for Leipzig was winding down, an escaped French prisoner made contact with Lieutenant Daniel Camous, a French officer attached to the American army. He led Camous to the suburb of Thekla, northeast of the city, and showed him a still smoldering, flattened barracks. It was what remained of a small labor camp that had supplied slaves for an aircraft factory near by. "Adjoining the Camp a few bodies of the political prisoners were laying on the field where they had been shot, trying to escape the barracks," Camous wrote in a report to the American command. "On the barbed wire some bodies (half burned and a look of terror on their faces) were stretched out. On the spot where the barracks used to be the remains of about 200 P[ersons] could be seen. The bodies had been shot and burnt beyond recognition."[9]

On April 24, the same day Camous filed his report, Major Richard J. Eaton of the American Military Government visited Thekla. "On April 16, or thereabouts," he wrote home, "about 60 men had been herded into one of the barracks, which was then set afire and the men burned alive." He wouldn't go into the "horrible details," he wrote, but when he returned to the United States he brought with him the snapshots he had taken.

Prisoners' remains at Thekla, snapshot by Richard J. Eaton.   (*USAMHI*)

Faced with such a scene, it was only natural that Eaton attempt to reconstruct in his mind what led to the calamity. He speculated that the workers must have tried to rebel as they heard the sounds of battle and the proximity of American troops. Thus he made a rational explanation—bodies near the fence were those of prisoners who tried to escape in the rebellion. The rest were herded into the barracks and burned as punishment. It was a gruesome enough tale, but what actually happened was worse. There had been no rebellion, no escape attempt, no reason at all for this final atrocity. The camp commandant had received orders to remove the prisoners from the reach of advancing American units, and as a result 1200 men and women, most sick and starving, were put on trucks and taken away (presumably to their deaths). That left more than 300 prisoners who would not fit onto the trucks or who were too sick to be transported.[10]

The evacuation took place on April 15th. The next day those who remained were lured into one of the barracks with big pots of soup. The SS then locked the doors and nailed heavy army blankets over the windows. Finally they brought up large containers of flammable acetate, opened the two doors and doused the interior and the prisoners with the chemical, locked the doors, and ignited the building with rifle fire and hand grenades. The barracks became an inferno. About a hundred, attempting to escape the blaze, burst out with bodies afire only to find the SS ready with guns and bazookas. A few got to the latrine trench, where they were beaten to death. More were impaled and machine-gunned on the fence. In the confusion, some escaped to an adjacent field, only to be cut down by a Hitler Youth squad manning tank machine guns. Somehow a handful of the original group survived, including the Frenchman who had led Daniel Camous to the scene.

Margaret Bourke-White of *Life* was among the first reporters to view Thekla, its ruins and corpses left undisturbed pending autopsies and press coverage. The terrible charred bodies, caught in motion as they fled the flames and rifle fire, etched the tragedy of individual humans in a manner different from what was observed at the larger camps. "Some of the victims were so close to freedom," Bourke-White recalled soon after, "that it made my

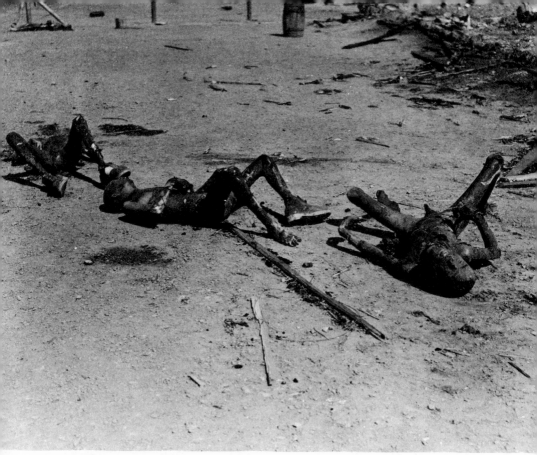

Thekla.

heart bleed to see them." She was told of the Polish professor who
had been an aircraft technician (and the survivors pointed him
out)—his body aflame, still he had managed to squeeze himself
halfway through the outer fence. "The shriveled lower half of his
body lay in cinders within the enclosure," she wrote, "with his
charred crutch close by, but the fine intellectual bald head thrust
through to the outside was still unmarred, with even the spectacles
in place. He must have been much loved; the survivors shed many
tears over him." Another man's blistered body had a silver cross
around its neck. A returned survivor of Thekla knelt down, touched
the medal, and said, "Blood on the cross."[11]

The American Military Government charged the mayor of
Leipzig with requisitioning coffins and laborers in order to con-
struct a proper burial for the victims, the site for which lay within

Thekla.

the main cemetery of the city. Major Eaton described the ceremony in a letter home:

> A chaplain made the actual arrangements for the services which were simple and impressive. He transported over 100 D.P.s [displaced persons] of four or five nationalities representing those of the victims, the city providing suitable clothing for them. A guard of honor of three G.I.s headed the procession from the main gate, then three chaplains (Jewish, Catholic, Protestant), then the D.P.s carrying garlands and bouquets, then six U.S. officers, then the civilians headed by the Burgo and his 100 leading citizens in morning dress and silk hats. In addition, nearly 1000 other citizens were present to represent a cross-section of the population. The procession marched to the burial place where the three chaplains took over (none too briefly). Taps were

blown (exceedingly well from the chapel steps at the end of the allee). The D.P.s laid their flowers on the graves and the people moved off in the same order as they came in. Not a sound from anybody except the chaplains for a half hour. The Burgomeister quite evidently had the support of the city in doing the job well. Everything was neat as a pin at the cemetery, the soil neatly piled and covered with green branches, the wreaths carefully made and fresh, the congregation serious. There was not the slightest disturbance.[12]

Eaton was deeply moved by the ceremony, especially by the effort and respect displayed by the citizens of Leipzig. "I think the people of the city were shocked by the tragedy, when they heard of it," he told his wife, "and were quite willing to express themselves by cooperating with sincerity. One wonders how much they knew of the horrors of the Hitler regime. If they did know and approved of them then they are more consummate and artful deceivers

Two survivors of Thekla view the remains of their fellow prisoners, April 20, 1945.

than seems humanly possible." He admitted that he might be "soft and stupid about them," but he could not imagine that the people he had been meeting all week were scoundrels. "Some are, of course," he admitted, "but 99 out of 100 of the average citizens seem to eat and breathe as we do, seem to react to the same emotions, seem to be perfectly human and responsive."[13]

Eaton was no doubt correct in his assessment, but it only served to beg the question. It is clear that Leipzig citizens, while horrified by the spectacularly cruel massacre at Thekla, certainly knew of the existence of the labor camps per se. German laborers worked in the same factories as the inmates; the citizenry watched them march back and forth from work. All over Germany, concentration camps, labor camps, and Kommandos made plain the exploitation of foreign and German men and women in forced labor. It is possible or even probable that many or most did not know and even tried hard to avoid learning what went on behind the barbed wire, but the smoke and smell of the crematorium often dropped unavoidable hints.

The discoveries continued. The Sixth Armored Division found a small camp at Penig, one filled with Hungarian Jewish women suffering from hunger, tuberculosis, typhus, gangrene, and other diseases. The Americans brought them to a former Luftwaffe hospital and forced German nurses and doctors to treat the survivors. And in the Bavarian Forest, along the Czech border and far from any sizable city, the 90th Infantry discovered Flossenburg, a major concentration camp. On April 19, just a week before the liberation, the Nazis had executed Pastor Dietrich Bonhoeffer at Flossenburg. The day before the liberation they force marched 15,000 prisoners to other camps, though many met death along the way. When the Americans arrived, two thousand of the sickest prisoners were there to greet them. In the area around Flossenburg, American soldiers discovered mass graves. To all this the local inhabitants swore ignorance.[14]

Bergen-Belsen was in a class by itself. Located in the countryside near Hanover, it began as a specialty camp in the SS empire, one where privileged prisoners and especially those Jews who might be bartered for money or goods were kept. By early 1944

Liberated Hungarian Jew,
Penig, April 17, 1945.

Corpses being taken out of Flossenburg for proper burial, May 3, 1945.

German civilians forced to view some of the eight hundred corpses found near Namering. Prisoners had been on a death march from Flossenburg.

GIs inspect victims of death march from Flossenburg.

American soldier tells German civilians about Flossenburg death march.

Belsen had expanded to become a less exclusive transit camp for evacuees from the overrun camps in the East. Its special population was being outnumbered by thousands of sick and dying transported prisoners. The final great wave came in early 1945, when the Nazis shipped a good part of the population of Auschwitz to Belsen's already overcrowded barracks. And with these prisoners came the typhus bug. With little or no food or potable water, and typhus running rampant, Belsen became an uncontrollable nightmare of death and depravity. Yet the transports still arrived, and the population of the camp swelled to 60,000 by the first week of April. In the ensuing two weeks 28,000 more prisoners arrived. Five hundred inmates were dying every day. The Nazis cut off the food supply entirely, signs of cannibalism began to appear, and the camp sank into a swamp of death and dissolution.

Belsen was in the British area of operations, and after some negotiations the Germans agreed to transfer the camp's operation to the British without a battle. Awe-struck by the awful challenge that faced them, British officers began clean-up and rehabilitation operations. Mass graves started by the Germans were filled and new ones dug. Distribution of food and water and medical aid to the forty or more thousand living souls began. But even so, day after day hundreds died from the raging typhus epidemic. It is estimated that, despite the best efforts of the British to feed and treat the inmates, some 28,000 died after the liberation.[15]

Curtis Mitchell was one of the few Americans to visit the camp in its first days of British control. Mitchell had been more familiar than most with the camps, since his job was to screen Signal Corps photos for public release, and he had already viewed pictures from the camps liberated early in April. He had flown to Paris to help coordinate the photographic record of American operations in Germany, but when he heard about the takeover of

Photograph by Curtis Mitchell of mass grave at Bergen-Belsen.

Survivors at Belsen, April 1945.

Belsen by the British on April 15, he rushed off with a photographer to see the camp.[16]

Mitchell's tour began at the deceptively attractive main gate, but soon he drove down the rows of barracks and experienced his first shock. At each barracks door lay a pile of bodies. A British soldier in a high-bed truck, commanding two Nazi soldiers, stopped at each door and the two German prisoners heaved the bodies one at a time into the truck. He watched as the bodies flew through the air and disappeared onto the truck bed, the Germans acting "just as if they were dumping garbage." His British guide took him into a barracks. When they entered, animal cries pierced the silence and the floors of a room that held over a hundred prisoners were filled with men crawling toward the Britisher and the American in the hope that they had food. They had none, the barracks quieted down, and Mitchell could hear only the steady drip of excrement from one

The mass grave at Belsen viewed by Curtis Mitchell.

tier of bunks to the next and to the ground.[17]

Finally, Mitchell was taken to see the mass graves. He watched at first from a distance as soldiers took one body after another and tossed them over an embankment. Then he walked to the edge of the pit, a hole thirty by fifty by ten feet made for 5000 bodies, and peered down. He froze into numbness. "I didn't feel anything at all except Jesus Christ Jesus Christ Jesus Christ and I kept saying that to myself because I couldn't think of anything else." But soon Mitchell, like others before him in similar situations, chillingly but necessarily walled himself off from what he was witnessing: ". . . [Y]ou got over feeling that these were people any more. They were so thin and so dried out that they might have been monkeys or plaster of Paris and you had to keep saying to yourself, these are human beings, and even when you said it your mind was not believing it because nothing like this had ever happened before and it just couldn't happen."[18]

5 | Dachau

In the heady days before World War I, when the city-dweller in Munich wished to escape the bustle of Bavaria's capital and cultural center, when even the park at Nymphenburg with its rococo buildings and formal garden seemed too much, he or she could take the train north eleven miles to the country town of Dachau. It had its own modest but picturesque *Schloss,* a small (5800 inhabitants) and quiet village, and offered soothing vistas of the countryside with Munich in the distance. The *Dachauer Moos,* a marsh plain that spread out south of the town had become the inspiration to a "Dachau school" of landscape painters enchanted by the gentle greens and yellows that shimmered in the misty light. An American soldier entering the town in April 1945 could still be impressed by its peaceful demeanor. "There are flower beds and trees," wrote Marcus J. Smith about his arrival, "small shops, bicycles on the ground, churches with steeples, a mirrorlike river. . . ." The scene yielded no hint of the madness that lay just minutes down the road. In just twelve years that madness, the concentration camp of Dachau, had immortalized the name of a thousand-year-old town.[1]

Dachau was the pilot camp of the Nazi regime, founded in 1933 to intern and "reeducate" Communists, Social Democrats, and others who voiced opposition to Hitler. In a short time it gained the reputation for grim labor and sadism. Then, after the terror of *Kristallnacht* in November 1938, more than 13,000 Jews were sent to Dachau and received punishment even more severe than that meted out to the political prisoners. Most of the Jews were released after they handed over a great deal of money and property to the SS and pledged to emigrate; still, in the few months that this large group resided at the camp more than seven hundred died. The few who did survive but could not secure their liberty eventually perished at Auschwitz or other extermination centers in the East.

Dachau, the name meant to strike terror in the minds of those who considered opposing the Nazis, found its reputation changing during the war. Much like Buchenwald, especially in the grapevine of the camp prisoners themselves, it came to be considered a mild camp. Actually it was probably even more benign than Buchenwald, for Dachau's work details were usually less demanding than the quarry work and tunnel building expected of *Kommandos* around Weimar. Not that Dachau was a gentle place. Hunger, disease, hard labor, and death were everyday affairs. The SS used the camp as a site for hangings and firing squads, and even built a gas chamber on the premises. Nazi doctors also made Dachau a center for medical experiments, using men, women, and children prisoners to test products and techniques for German manufacturers and the German military. For instance, a Doctor Schilling infected about 1100 prisoners, many of them Polish priests, with malaria in order to observe malarial behavior and to try out cures. A Doctor Rascher used prisoner guinea-pigs in experiments to find out what happened to pilots when they lost cabin pressure and oxygen at high altitudes. Rascher also carried out other experiments: to find out how to warm up pilots shot down over the ocean and exposed to near-freezing water temperatures; to determine the physical effects of drinking sea water. In all cases the experiments led to death or horrible pain for those involved.[2]

As at most camps, over time the conditions at Dachau changed for the worse as the war effort demanded ever more slave labor and as the killing of Jews became of prime importance to the Nazis by the end of 1941. Dachau then became a hub for the shipment of slave workers and prisoners there often witnessed the dire results of the transportation system. In November 1942, for instance, a trainload of 900 laborers transferred from Mauthausen experienced such misery on the train that most died within a few days after arriving at Dachau. In that same month a transport from Danzig arrived with three hundred dead, mostly victims of exposure and starvation. Some of the corpses bore the traces of cannibalism. The survivors soon died as well. Near the end of the war, a train from Buchenwald estimated to be carrying 5000 prisoners arrived with only 1200 survivors. Some were so thirsty that they drank water continuously and died as a result. These are but a few examples of the transports that Dachau received throughout the war. It was as if the system of exploitation and extermination which Dachau had begun had come home to roost.[3]

For the most part, Dachau had been able to absorb these shipments and retain a semblance of order. But in the last months of the war, with supply lines endangered, and the arrival of ever increasing trainloads of disease-ridden prisoners, the camp began its inevitable slide into uncontrolled death and decay. By late April of 1945, perhaps even more than at Buchenwald, Dachau was in reality two camps. There remained a sizable contingent of its older population, healthy enough to work and even to organize themselves. But all around them lay the dead and dying human cargo from other camps, the telling remains of the slave labor and extermination efforts of the concentration camp system as a whole. The crematoria worked overtime, mass burial sites were opened to deal with the overflow, but there seemed no end to the transports and to wholesale death.

On the morning of April 29th, men of the 45th Division's 157th Infantry Regiment and supporting armor launched a three-pronged attack on Munich. One company got as far as the small town of Prittlbach, adjacent to the town of Dachau, but found that all the bridges across a canal that bordered Dachau had been blown up. The attack on Munich seemed stymied. With no quick solution in sight, soldiers questioned a woman on a bicycle only to find that she had just come from Munich across a bridge in the town of Dachau itself. Mounting the tanks, the infantrymen retraced her route in a sudden and unanticipated move through the town. Just as the lead tank got to the bridge, the Germans managed to blow it up. The infantrymen found a small footbridge across the canal and the advance continued. One of their objectives along the way to Munich was the Dachau concentration camp, and they now headed in its direction.

Coming from the other side of town at about the same time, members of the 42nd Division's 222nd Infantry Regiment also had received orders to move on the camp. Ahead of the main body of the 222nd, a caravan of three jeeps carrying, among others, the journalist Marguerite Higgins and General Henning Linden, raced toward Dachau's main gate. It had been rumored that a group of special prisoners including Stalin's son, the French politician Léon Blum, and Austria's ex-chancellor Kurt Schuschnigg were being held at Dachau. The army wanted to rescue them, and Higgins wanted a scoop.

At first it seemed that taking the camp would be as militarily uneventful as other concentration camp liberations. Intelligence reports had assured the 45th and 42nd Divisions that the camp was being defended by members of the ragtag *Volkssturm,* a militia recruited in the desperation of defeat and rarely known to put up much of a fight. Instead, on the way to the camp both groups of GIs had encountered small but hardnosed units of SS and they expected much resistance at the camp itself.

It was in this battle-ready frame of mind that several units converged on the railroad siding that serviced the camp, there to find about forty open freight cars filled with more than 2000 corpses, the tangle of bodies laced with ragged remnants of striped uniforms and the stench of excrement and death. "Some turned their heads, white-faced and sick," the official report said of the GIs. "Others with horrible fascination looked at the pile of dead." Combat veterans wept, stared with sullen moveless faces, and anger sharpened their already edgy nerves. From various directions men from the 45th and then from the 42nd rushed the interior of the camp and came upon more grim scenes. Corpses littered the camp, but no sight save the train compared with the neatly stacked bodies outside the crematorium.

Hitler Youth being shown boxcars at Dachau.

GI at the boxcars, Dachau.

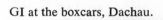

(Witness to the Holocaust)

Well you were just in a state of shock really, nobody had ever seen anything like that before. You know, I had been in the service and I had seen men die before. I've seen dead bodies, but not stacked up like cordwood. —Bill Allison, 14th Armored Division[4]

The first thing I saw was a stack of bodies that appeared to be about, oh, 20 feet long and about, oh, as high as a man could reach, which looked like cordwood stacked up there, and the thing I'll never forget was the fact that closer inspection found people whose eyes were still blinking maybe three or four deep inside the stack. —Jack Hallett, a liberator of Dachau[5]

Well after seeing the train and then standing there looking through that fence at these people, you couldn't believe what you saw. It gave you a lost, sick feeling . . . Well, it's haunted me as I say for 36 years. I mean, who are they? What's their name? What nationality are they? What is their religious faith? Why were they there? You just can't comprehend it. —Henry Dejarnette, a liberator of Dachau[6]

The need to comprehend what they saw, the desire to make some order in their minds of the chaos around them, sometimes made GIs fix on one part of the whole. That could mean simply focusing on a stack of bodies that had the order of cordwood. For others, concentrating on one exceptional victim helped to humanize the scene. One liberator could still remember a "real good looking red-headed lady" in one of the piles of bodies. A soldier who visited the camp a week after liberation apparently saw the same pile and his way of humanizing the experience was to concentrate on a "two-foot-square portion of this 'monument of the dead.' " In that jumbled area he focused on a "beautiful Polish girl," the distorted features of a dead Russian, and the "finely combed reddish-brown coiffure of yet another young woman." By creating some order in his mind, he was able to control his reactions to a scene made more frightening because of its disorder.[7]

In any case, the combination of confusion and anger at seeing these atrocities and the fact that the soldiers were still in a

Survivors of Dachau, April 30, 1945.

combat situation encouraged the unleashing of revenge on the remaining SS as they were captured. Such violence reached its peak when angry members of a squad guarding 122 captured Germans opened machine-gun fire and killed them all. When seen from the distance of four decades, this and other such incidents sometimes elicited a burning sense of guilt. One liberator talked about having problems sleeping when he thought about Dachau, but the memories were mostly of the "atrocities that were committed in the camp . . . by our people." The violence of Dachau had a way of implicating all, even the liberators.[8]

Ex-prisoners at Dachau taunting a captured guard. In background are German guards killed by U.S. Army personnel.

> Control was gone after the sights we saw, and the men were deliberately wounding guards that were available and then turned them over to the prisoners and allowing them to take their revenge on them. And in fact, you've seen the picture where one of the soldiers gave one of the inmates a bayonet and watched him behead the man. It was a pretty gory mess. A lot of the guards were shot in the legs so they couldn't move and . . . and that's about all I can say . . .
> —Jack Hallett[9]

Balanced against scenes of death and revenge were outbursts of joy that greeted the Americans. Prisoners hoisted their liberators in triumph and carried them across the parade ground; other prisoners kissed and cheered the surprised and unnerved GIs in celebration of their miraculous reprieve from certain death. Somehow the prisoners had even managed to make an American flag, which they waved in delirium. Soon the walls of the barracks had been painted with triumphant slogans. But even these celebrations were marked with the inevitable and inescapable truths of Dachau. The cheering crowds were also carrying bodies of captured SS guards, which they were ripping apart limb by limb. One celebrant became so excited that he bolted from his barracks and was electrocuted on the live wires of the fence.

For every cheering prisoner healthy enough to show his appreciation, there were many more who were too weak and even close to death. "They'd be sitting, just squatting down," a liberator remembered. "We walked up and they'd say, 'Amerikanish?' We'd say 'Yeah.' And some of them would get up. Stand up. And some would fall back down. . . . They were skin and bones."[10]

The Americans witnessed all this in their first hour at Dachau—tears, anger, violence, joy, and revenge. The whole range of emotions surfaced again and again as new troops entered the camp, as new prisoners were made aware of the Americans, as some previously unnoticed SS sniped at a GI or into the crowd of prisoners, or some other guard was discovered in hiding and killed.

Amidst this cacophony unfolded a strange drama at the front gate of the camp. Lieutenant Felix Sparks of the 157th's 3rd Battalion, the group that had entered the camp first, was finally getting some order established. Sparks, who had been commanded by his superiors to seal off the camp—to let no one in or out—was near the main gate when General Linden, Marguerite Higgins, and the supporting jeeps from the 222nd pulled up. The General told Sparks that Higgins wanted to interview the special prisoners in the camp. While Sparks informed the General that he had orders to keep the camp shut, the reporter ran to the gate, already covered with a crowd of inmates pressing their faces to the bars. As Higgins reached the entrance, the prisoners surged forward in an enthusiastic mass. Sparks's men had to fire their rifles over the heads of the prisoners to restore order.[11]

Dachau liberated.

Liberation day at Dachau.

Sparks, already at the breaking point from the events of the past hour, brusquely asked the General and his jeeps to leave and assigned a man to show them the way. As Sparks's man approached General Linden's jeep, the General took his riding crop and hit the GI on his helmet. Sparks cursed the General and verbally threatened to remove his group by force. When Linden tried to relieve Sparks of his command, Sparks drew his pistol and forced him to leave, but not before the General threatened to bring Sparks before a court-martial.[12]

After the General drove away, things began to settle down. Members of the 42nd and 45th Divisions shared guard and supervisory duties for a day, and then most were replaced by other units as the push toward Munich continued. But for most there was at least time for a cursory tour of the camp. The inmates were only too happy to oblige, showing their liberators the crematoria, torture instruments, barracks, and other landmarks. One important stop on the tour became notably controversial among the inmates and liberators alike. The gas chamber, which had been built in 1942, had the usual Nazi ruse, *Brausebad* [shower bath], marked on its heavy steel door. The GIs were shown the facility, but different inmates gave different accounts of its use. Some said it was in operation constantly, others said it had been used only occasionally. Still others insisted that it had never been used at all. The difference of opinion as well as the gas chamber itself were two of the more unsettling details of the GIs' brief stay at Dachau.[13]

Those who liberated the camp and those who took over administration of its survivors were so incensed by what they had found that they published a report on Dachau, the camp and the town, that combined the findings of Office of Strategic Services, Counterintelligence Corps, and other units. In addition to a history of the camp and a description of conditions before and after the liberation, the booklet included the diary of a prisoner and other testimony of survivors.

One chapter of the pamphlet dealt with a question much on the minds of GIs in the area. What of the citizens of Dachau? What did they know? What did they do? After extensive interviews with townspeople, the army investigators concluded that *"Was*

Part of the tour at Dachau.

konnten wir tun?" [What could we do?] seemed to be the response most often heard. Many claimed anti-Nazi feelings, but felt terrorized themselves and unable to do anything about the camp. Josef Scherrer was typical of this group. He had so antagonized the authorities that only having a powerful friend prevented his arrest by the SS. Silence became the price of freedom. Others, noted the interviewers, didn't really care about the prisoners at the camp "as long as business was good and the SS *Hauptsturmfuhrer* paid his handsome rent," and they were usually the ones who pleaded: *"Ja—wir wussten uberhaupt nichts was passiert da draussen!"* [We really didn't know what was going on out there!] But these sorts, according to the army's report, were relatively few in number.

Cover of Dachau pamphlet.

(*Witness to the Holocaust*)

Even fewer were those who showed open opposition, and they sometimes were able to remain anti-Nazis only because their business dealings were away from the town or because they traveled. In fact, the army interviewers thought that they sometimes had it easier than those who remained quiet:

> Herr Engelhard, for example, worked for a firm which sent him travelling over all Southern Europe. Herr Grasal had a small importing business from Italy. They could both afford to isolate themselves (as they did) in their houses for years. Herr Grasal—who is obviously the type who likes his Gemutlichkeit—said that he had never gone into a tavern for years for fear he "might talk *too* freely." He gave up all entertaining seven years ago. By contrast Herr Scherrer, who was not so extreme in his remarks, emerges as a man who has suffered far more and who had every bit as much courage. He made his living by running a restaurant. For a known anti-Nazi in a town which was a Nazi "Hochburg" and a cradle of the SS this is no small achievement. "Meine Nerven sind vollkommen zur Grunde gegangen," he says. [My nerves are totally shot.] Small wonder.[14]

The assessment of Dachau's citizenry ended on a rather conciliatory note, warning against judging a whole town and reminding the reader of the "fearsome shadow" that hung over everyone "in a state in which crime ha[d] been incorporated and called the government."[15]

How, after all, could one judge these people? They lived in a different universe from the camp, and the connection between town and camp became more tenuous with every new interview, with every attempt to assess responsibility. No matter that Dachau's prisoners and camp had been an integral factor of the town's growth and prosperity, that all the citizenry of Dachau lived within the camp's orbit. The two worlds were connected in ways unrevealed by interviews. Yet frightening in its very human dimension was the fact that army officers, outraged by what they had seen in the camp, still seemed more able to comprehend the moral dilemmas of Dachau's citizenry than they ever would be able to understand the ghastly histories of those they liberated.

6 | Mauthausen

After the unimaginable sights of Ohrdruf, Buchenwald, Dachau, and the others, it would be hard to believe that some new level of horror might be reached. Yet on May 5, as the American 11th Armored Division and other units reconnoitered along the Danube in the environs of Linz, Austria, they found at the "mother" concentration camp of Mauthausen and such satellite camps as Gusen, Ebensee, and Gunskirchen, new histories and varieties of death and degradation. Indeed, Mauthausen and its branches had a reputation among prisoners, from Dachau in the West to Auschwitz in the East, as the camp to avoid at all costs.

The history of Mauthausen dated from 1938, when Heinrich Himmler sought to expand the economic base of the SS by exploiting slave labor in the extractive and manufacturing industries. He needed new camps and new business opportunities. Soon after the *Anschluss* that made Austria a part of Germany, he chose a site near the village of Mauthausen which offered a combination of attractive features. The future camp would be built next to the Wienergraben, a municipal quarry which was a principal supplier of paving stones for Vienna and other cities and thus had a secure economic future. The quarry was located in isolated farm country, but near enough to Linz to be useful. Mauthausen also was a stop on a railway line, thus easing both transport of stone and labor.[1]

By July 1938 prisoners from Dachau were leveling the ground for a complex planned to cover almost four square miles, more than a square mile of which was quarry. Three months later the first inmates arrived, about a thousand German political prisoners with a sprinkling of others. A year later the prisoner population had grown over two and a half times; SS statistics listed, among the major groups, 688 political prisoners, 143 Jehovah's Witnesses and other religious objectors, 51 homosexuals, 930 asocials (a catchall category), and 946 criminals. This last category was of particular importance, for German criminals supplied the SS with cruel prisoner-taskmasters who sometimes exceeded the Nazis themselves in sadism. As the years passed, the camp kept expanding its barracks and administrative facilities.[2]

Mauthausen shared with other concentration camps the usual array of atrocities: medical experiments, exterminations, torture, and the rest. But what set it apart from other camps—in fact what gave it its damning reputation among prisoners at Dachau, Buchenwald, and even Auschwitz—was its quarry. Stone cutting and hauling is an arduous occupation in the best of circumstances but, under the supervision of the SS, work at the Wienergraben became torture almost beyond belief. Slave laborers in the quarry had a life expectancy of between six weeks and three months, and that was the case only if an unplanned punishment did not get in the way. Though pneumatic tools were used and blasting was sometimes employed to loosen stone, most of the labor was with pick and axe. As for moving stone from the quarry, prisoners hauled heavy chunks of granite on their backs up 186 steep and narrow steps that connected the camp to the quarry.[3]

The quarry was the site of not only impossibly hard work, but also unspeakable sadism. Hundreds of Dutch Jews were forced to jump to their deaths from the high cliff overlooking the quarry floor, a cliff which in the grim humor of the inmates became known as the "parachutists' wall." In one instance, the SS orchestrated a blasting operation that made even jaded prisoners tremble. The Nazi officer in charge ordered an Italian Jew known to have a beautiful voice to stand atop a rock mound and sing the "Ave Maria." As he sang, charges were laid around the rocks. In midsong the officer pressed the plunger and blasted both the Jew and the rocks. Every day at the quarry brought new and novel forms of death.[4]

In addition, Mauthausen was one of the few camps in the West to employ its gas chamber regularly. At first a mobile gas van shuttled back and forth between the main camp and Gusen sub-camp. On each trip it killed thirty prisoners, and apparently was in constant use. By December 1941 a permanent gas chamber, one that could hold about 120 prisoners at a time, seems to have been put in operation. It was small by Nazi standards, and when large transports earmarked for extermination arrived at Mauthausen, most persons were sent to the larger facilities at nearby Hartheim Castle. It is estimated that between 1942 and 1945 a total of about 10,000 persons were executed in Mauthausen's gas chamber, at Hartheim Castle, and in the vans.[5]

As with the other camps, conditions at Mauthausen began to get even worse after 1943 with the movement of prisoners west from Poland. Mauthausen, because of the geographical proximity of Hungary, was particularly affected by the late but efficient roundup of that country's Jews. Especially after the evacuation of Auschwitz in December 1944, the Nazis sent thousands of Hungarian Jews to Mauthausen and its sub-camps. Marched through the winter with little clothing or food, those that survived to enter the camp gates were in desperate physical and psychological condition.[6]

In short, Mauthausen doubled as a profitable enterprise for the DEST (Deutsche Erd-und Steinwerke, or German Earth and Stone Works) and an alternative method of extermination to meet the SS's other goals. One estimate puts total deaths at Mauthausen between 1938 and 1945 at about 55,000, this out of a total prisoner population of about 185,000. But even these statistics are conservative, since they do not adequately take into account the reuse of prisoner numbers (more than one death occurring as represented by a prisoner number), the deaths of thousands of prisoners, especially at the end of the war, who were shipped to Mauthausen and died, and the number of prisoners at Mauthausen who were never properly registered.[7]

Nor does the human destruction that Mauthausen spawned appear in its true magnitude if one limits oneself to the "mother" camp alone, for radiating out of the main camp was an extensive system of brutal sub-camps. This kind of proliferation of labor camps was common enough in the system—Buchenwald, Dachau, and other centers had their own satellite operations—but none contained a more consistently cruel set of sub-camps than Mauthausen. The major ones were Gusen and Ebensee. Gusen, founded in 1940, was an independent camp until 1944, when it came under the umbrella of Mauthausen. Six kilometers west of the mother camp, it too specialized in quarry work. Inmates at Gusen and its sub-camps also built underground armaments factories for production of machine guns and other weaponry, as well as fuselages for Messerschmidt aircraft. In 1945 Gusen became an end-destination for death marches from other camps, and death lists from the Gusen camps add up to over 38,000. Ebensee was created in 1943 to provide labor for the construction of underground factory tunnels, but by 1945 had become a grisly center for dying transported prisoners.[8] In all there were close to fifty camps, big and small, that operated within Mauthausen's sphere of administration. They supplied labor for a wide variety of SS and privately owned industries, and were spread all over Austria.[9]

As Allied troops swept across most of Germany in March and April 1945, the SS had to decide what to do with Mauthausen. At first Himmler's order was to turn it over to the Allies intact, but that was soon countermanded by more sinister plans to destroy the camp, sub-camps, and the prisoners that were left. The second plan was never put into operation. In late April, Nazi Commandant Ziereis handed over administration of the camp to a captain in the Vienna police, leaving a small group of SS to help guard the camp. Underground groups in Mauthausen proper as well as at Gusen quickly began sabotage and resistance operations, but the sad fact was that what was needed most—food, medicine, clothing, and final liberation—had to await the arrival of American forces some days later. Until then the camps festered in dirt and disease. Thousands of prisoners died. Conditions were especially appalling among the latest transported prisoners. These men and women had survived Auschwitz, Dachau, and forced marches—only to perish at Mauthausen in the final week of the war.

View of Gusen.

The dead at Gusen.

Woman survivor of Gusen.

Local citizens load bodies for burial, Gusen.   (*Witness to the Holocaust*)

It was, above all, these last arrivals that shocked the Americans as they entered Mauthausen and its sub-camps on May 5 and the days that followed. The knowledge that such camps existed, that in the previous month thousands of GIs had seen similar scenes, did nothing to lessen the impact. Here were human beings—dead, close to death, wandering in a haze, starved and beaten into a chilling sameness—naked and semi-naked and in any case stripped of all the things we rely upon to identify someone as human. Here the Americans responded in much the same way their fellow soldiers had in other camps. There seemed to be no limit to how bad conditions could get, only to how one could react. "When you see them," one GI remembered, "there is nothing to distinguish them, you know. Shaved heads and sunken cheeks . . . there is no way,

The banner text reads:

SALUDAN A LAS FUERZAS LIBERADORAS
ИСПАНСКИЕ АНТИФАШИСТЫ
ПРИВЕТСТВУЮТ ОСВОБОДИТЕЛЕЙ

11th Armored Division cheered at Mauthausen, May 9, 1945. The banner was created by Spanish Loyalist prisoners.

Ex-prisoners at Mauthausen tear down Eagle and Swastika, May 6, 1945.

Crippled survivors at Mauthausen, May 6, 1945.

it is hard to even see them as human. Under the circumstances you try to avoid seeing them too much. It is too hard to do. It is too hard to handle."[10]

Indeed Mauthausen, like the other camps, was the stuff of which nightmares are made. George E. King was probably not alone in feeling victimized by his very presence in the camp, even as a liberator. He described one of his dreams: "You are the captured. And you go through this agonizing labor of trying to escape. In these cases you are always moving in slow motion, as if you were up to your hips in mud . . . you are making a maximum effort to run, but you are just barely moving. . . ." The fear of becoming one of the prisoners; assuaging guilt over not being one by joining the imprisoned in one's dreams; being tortured by the memory of all that surrounded one—these were some of the dreadful themes that only sometimes surfaced in the conscious or even dream world of the liberator.[11]

Those Americans who entered Mauthausen, like GIs at other camps, sometimes exhibited strongly contradictory urges to remember and to forget. Franklin Clark felt he must photograph what he saw, and he wanted his wife to see the pictures as well. When he sent them to her, he asked her to burn them. "I didn't want them around," he recalled. "I didn't even want to be reminded of them." Yet finally he kept them.[12]

Others seemingly had no conflict about remembering their experience and informing others. Like the Seventh Army at Dachau, the 71st Division, which liberated the sub-camp of Gunskirchen, published a small pamphlet of text, photographs, and drawings to convince those who read it of the reality of the experience: *The Seventy-First Came . . . to Gunskirchen Lager*.[13] Gunskirchen Lager had been the destination for transports of Hungarian Jews, who once totaled 17,000 at the sub-camp. Only 5000 were alive when the 71st came upon the site. In one barracks there were 2600 people. "Filth all over," read the report of one medical doctor. "No water, no heating, no light, no food. About 500 bodies lying in the area. The living bodies were skin and bones. People full of lice and dirt."[14]

Mauthausen, May 5, 1945.

Mauthausen, May 5, 1945.

Capt. J. D. Pletcher described Gunskirchen the morning of its discovery:

"Of all the horrors of the place, the smell, perhaps, was the most startling of all. It was a smell made up of all kinds of odors—human excreta, foul bodily odors, smoldering trash fires, German tobacco—which is a stink in itself—all mixed together in a heavy dank atmosphere, in a thick, muddy woods, where little breeze could go. The ground was pulpy throughout the camp, churned to a consistency of warm putty by the milling of thousands of feet, mud mixed with feces and urine. The smell of Gunskirchen

119

THE SEVENTY-FIRST CAME... TO GUNSKIRCHEN LAGER

(*Witness to the Holocaust*)

Cover of Gunskirchen pamphlet.

nauseated many of the Americans who went there. It was a smell I'll never forget, completely different from anything I've ever encountered. It could almost be seen and hung over the camp like a fog of death.

As we entered the camp, the living skeletons still able to walk crowded around us and, though we wanted to drive farther into the place, the milling, pressing crowd wouldn't let us. It is not an exaggeration to say that almost every inmate was insane with hunger. Just the sight of an American brought cheers, groans, and shrieks. People crowded around to touch an American, to touch the jeep, to kiss our arms—perhaps just to make sure that it was true. The people who couldn't walk crawled out toward our jeep. Those who couldn't even crawl propped themselves up on an elbow, and somehow, through all their pain and suffering, revealed through their eyes the gratitude, the joy they felt at the arrival of Americans."[15]

Survivors at Ebensee.

The situation at Ebensee was hardly better. Bodies, ashes, the living dead riddled the compound, and even those who could stand sometimes just collapsed and died. One liberator recalled giving showers to the survivors and watching one collapse from the shock of the water.

We were taken through the crematoriums—and one of the attendants of the crematorium swore to us that he had seen several bodies put in there alive. We looked in the crematorium and there were piles of ashes and bones inside. And outside of the crematoriums, the bodies were stacked like firewood—like hides and carcasses you see hanging of half a cow in a butcher shop—the spine, you could count every vertebra in the spine and every rib and these were the dead, but the living looked exactly like them. The living that were walking around were so gaunt; their heads were shaven; they had sores on their bodies. Some were walking around naked in a daze; others had blankets wrapped around them held together by a belt and their facial features were normal size, but everything else was completely out of proportion. —Bert Weston on conditions at Ebensee[16]

Survivor of Ebensee.

Ebensee, May 1945.

The conditions at Mauthausen and its satellite camps were so bad that every day hundreds continued to die from exhaustion, dehydration, starvation, typhus, and tuberculosis. Americans witnessed these crushing scenes of death and human degradation even as millions of men and women safe in America danced wildly in the streets in celebration of V-E Day. The prisoners presented their own victory ceremony, with Allied officials and camp inmates present. The liberators at Mauthausen cheered, though with the muting knowledge of human carnage all around them. As for the liberated, some celebrated, others tried, and still others hardly knew what had happened before they perished.

Liberated prisoners at Ebensee, May 7, 1945.

Survivors of Ebensee.

7 | Telling the Story

Percy Knauth said it about Buchenwald, but it was true of all the camps: "You just can't understand it, even when you've seen it."[1] An expression of shock and horror, his pronouncement also alluded to a central problem confronting liberators. The sights and smells of the liberated camps were hard enough to grasp and assimilate when on the scene. It would be difficult in the extreme to convey that reality second-hand to those at home. In the days that followed the liberations, both ex-prisoners and Allied governments engaged in extended efforts to make the camps and their story available to officials and newspersons. Newspaper stories, magazine articles, and newsreels flooded the West in April and May, depicting the camps as they had been discovered. The public response was marked for the most part by surprise and great outrage. At the same time, though the pictorial material alone made clear that there had been no exaggeration in the stories of Nazi wartime atrocities, the information campaign in general elicited reactions that indicated a continuing reluctance on the part of some individuals to confront the awful truth.

The attempt to transform an anarchy of bodies and ashes and living dead into some order actually began with the liberated prisoners themselves. During their captivity, individuals sometimes took great risks by preserving diaries, works of art, stolen official records, and other documents of their ordeal that the Nazis would have otherwise destroyed. After liberation, they aided army intelligence officers in putting together histories and descriptions of the

127

camps. Most of all, in virtually every camp, prisoner guides eagerly showed the highlights to arriving troops, dignitaries, and press persons: crematoria, mass graves, instruments of torture, gas chambers, and the endless personal stories of sacrifice and heroism that had given some meaning to existence for the prisoners themselves. Inevitably the biases of the guides entered into such presentations, especially in regard to rivalries between national groups and an endemic disdain for fellow prisoners who were Jews or Gypsies. Nonetheless the guides and the prisoner committees that surfaced in the first days after liberation gave a much needed form to the terrible scenes encountered in the first moments of entry into the camps.

Buchenwald and later Dachau became focal points for official tours. Each had a prisoner population well enough organized to tell the story and present a repertoire of sights vivid enough to change the mind of anyone who still doubted the reality of published reports. At Buchenwald visitors passed neatly stacked piles of bodies, visited the still inhabited barracks of the Little Camp, and filed by a table featuring a sample of items representative of the special sadistic tendencies of the staff: tattooed human skin collected by the ex-commandant's wife, Ilse Koch; shrunken heads of prisoners used as trophies and paperweights; pickled human organs collected by various SS officers in bogus medical experiments. At both Buchenwald and Dachau, the corpses outside of the crematoria and (in the case of Dachau) the train filled with bodies remained untouched for days while visitors inspected it. Only when such displays began to pose serious health problems were they removed. By any normal standard these were bizarre and ghoulish presentations, but it is also clear that any less graphic tour would not have had a lasting impact.

The tour of liberated concentration camps, in fact, became a ritual of exorcism and revelation in the occupied Germany of late April and early May 1945. Generals Patton and Eisenhower ordered every soldier in the area not committed to the front line to visit the camps. So few Germans admitted to knowing anything about the camps that American officers in charge made it a practice to force local citizens to view them. Finally a long stream of official

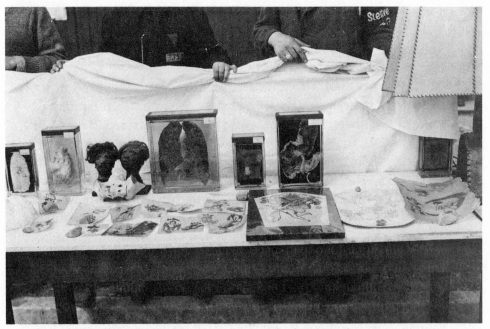

Display table at Buchenwald, showing shrunken heads, lampshades and other items of tattooed human skin, and preserved organs collected by SS.

Weimar citizens forced to view Buchenwald.

visitors began to answer Eisenhower's call for witnesses to the horrors.[2]

Congress quickly chose a bipartisan joint committee to tour the sites of the camps. It was headed by Senator Alben Barkley of Kentucky. Others from the Senate included Leverett Saltonstall of Massachusetts, Walter F. George of Georgia, Kenneth Wherry of Nebraska, Elbert Thomas of Utah, and C. Wayland Brooks of Illinois. The House was represented by John Vorys of Ohio, Ewing Thomason of Texas, James P. Richards of South Carolina, Ed Izac of California, James Mott of Oregon, and Dewey Short of Missouri. The committee left Washington on April 22 and arrived at Buchenwald on April 24; on May 1 they inspected the remains of Nordhausen and especially the V-1 and V-2 factories; and on May 2 they took in Dachau, liberated after they had arrived in Europe. In each camp they were given what would become the routine tour, including a spray of D.D.T. to prevent the spread of typhus. They were duly shocked by the conditions, and Representative Izac compiled a sixteen-page report to Congress: "Atrocities and Other Conditions in Concentration Camps in Germany." The report gave background material on the tour itself, reported briefly on the history and function of the camps, and then gave detailed descriptions of the three camps, the particulars gleaned from personal observation, interviews with survivors, and briefings given by army medical and intelligence officers. The committee concluded by endorsing the war crimes proceedings then under way and with the hope that out of the camp experience and trials of the guilty parties would emerge "a firmer realization that men of all nations and all tongues must resist encroachments of every theory and every ideology that debases mankind and that a more just and enduring peace may arise upon the ruins and from the sacrifices which the human race has endured through one of the most crucial periods of its history."[3]

In its organization, tone, and attention to numerical detail and description especially, the report managed both to confirm the existence of the camp system and its atrocities and to put the information in orderly and manageable form. It was praised for precisely these qualities.[4] Yet in so doing it reflected none of the

Congressman Ed Izac of California inspects human remains in oven.

Senator Alben Barkley views corpses at Buchenwald, April 24, 1945.

astonishment, none of the incomprehensibility, and none of the in-ability of eyewitnesses to cope with the whole of what they saw. It was only when the members of the committee shared their personal impressions with radio and lecture audiences that the sense of awe and disbelief emerged. And with it came the awkward language that attempted to cope with that reality. Representative John Vorys began one speech by assuring his listeners that he was "an eye-witness, an ear and nose witness . . . that the Nazi concentration camp story was true." He referred to the "ape-like living skeletons we saw," and noted later what to him seemed an inspiring contrast: "[The Buchenwald inmates] looked more like absent-minded apes in their striped prison suits and sunken eyes, although many were professors, doctors, writers, and generals. In talking with some of them who spoke English, what amazed me most, however was the way in which they had preserved their spirits and had not sunk mentally to the bestial level of their living."[5]

For most of the committee members, publicizing what they had seen was not only perceived as a moral duty, but also as good politics. In some cases, however, especially in states where there were large German-American populations, it was initially con-sidered a risk. Indeed, numerous constituents wrote to Senator Wherry expressing their fear that he might soft-pedal the sordid details of the camps in order not to alienate Nebraska's German-American voters. Wherry did quite the opposite, touring the state and making known his observations. In Omaha, according to one newspaper account, his audience "listened silently. Their lips were fixed. At intervals, they moved their heads in cold disbelief."[6]

In addition to the Congressional tour, Eisenhower also ar-ranged for a committee of distinguished American journalists under the leadership of Joseph Pulitzer to make a similar inspection. Pulitzer had harbored some doubt as to the authenticity of the first press reports about Ohrdruf, Buchenwald, and Nordhausen. "I came here," he wrote from Europe, "in a suspicious frame of mind, feeling that I would find that many of the terrible reports that have been printed in the United States before I left were exaggerations, and largely propaganda." After viewing the camps, he wrote of these reports: "They have been understatements."[7]

Congressional committee tours Buchenwald barracks: (*left to right*):
John Vorys (Ohio), Brig. Gen. John M. Weir, Col. William E. Williams,
Alben Barkley (Ky.), C. Wayland Brooks (Ill.), and Leverett Saltonstall
(Mass.), April 24, 1945.

Congressman Everett Dirksen is sprayed with DDT before entering Dachau,
May 12, 1945.

Pulitzer, as a German-American in the heavily German-American city of St. Louis, was so incensed by what he saw that he launched a campaign of public education, the need for which was underlined by the mood he detected upon his return home. "[T]here are still Americans," he wrote on May 20, 1945, "who are saying, in effect, 'this talk of atrocities is all propaganda. There may have been something wrong here and there but the German people would not stand for such things.' "[8] In cooperation with the federal government, Pulitzer's *St. Louis Post-Dispatch* mounted an exhibition of life-size photomurals made from Signal Corps photographs of the camps. "Lest We Forget," as the exhibition was titled, opened at the city's Kiel Auditorium, where more than 80,000 individuals jammed in to see it over a period of only twenty-five days. Coupled with the photo exhibit was a special, experimental showing of an hour-long motion picture documentary on the camps produced by the Signal Corps.

Editors, including Julius Ochs Adler of the *New York Times,* at Buchenwald.

Radio news commentators Lowell Thomas, Howard Barnes, and George Hamilton Combs view corpses at Buchenwald, April 18, 1945.

The film on the camps was, in fact, somewhat controversial. In the first days after the liberations the Signal Corps released graphic footage to the major newsreel companies to be shown in movie theatres as part of the weekly newsreel. The wisdom of showing these terrible scenes as part of the newsreels and, later, as a single film was questioned by some. They argued that such showings would only shock persons into a hatred of the German people, and that this sort of hatred only played into the worst excesses of Nazi ideology itself. It was a reasonable moral argument, but also one that seemed inspired, at least in part, by an unwillingness to confront the scenes themselves. A number of critics seemed unwilling to give up the label "propaganda" when dealing with human cruelty, even when it was the truth that was being shown.

This argument was particularly evident in James Agee's "review" of the atrocity films, which appeared in the *Nation* of May 19, 1945.[9] First, Agee attributed the showing of the films to "an ordered and successful effort to condition the people of this country against interfering with, or even questioning, an extremely hard peace against the people of Germany." He had "not felt it necessary to see the films themselves," he revealed, but he made it clear that his not having seen them should not disqualify his right to write about them. What followed was an essay on the dangers of vengeance and the possibility of confusing vengeance with justice. "Such propaganda" could only fuel this spirit, and allow us to confuse the German people with the few criminals who perpetuated the crimes. Furthermore, it would allow us the false pride of considering ourselves "incomparably their superiors" if our punishments stopped short of annihilation. He compared such an attitude toward the Germans to that of the mob in Milan that had hanged Mussolini and his mistress just weeks before. "Indeed, we are worse than they," Agee argued, "and worse in some respects, than the Nazis. There can be no bestiality so discouraging to contemplate as that of the man of good-will when he is misusing his heart and his mind. . . ."

Whatever the validity of Agee's general argument, it was one that assumed the effect such films might have on an audience. He might have felt differently had he seen them. If we are to judge public reaction by interviews with those emerging from viewings in St. Louis, a much more complex picture emerges. Certainly there was an inevitable disgust with the Germans and some call for punishment. "I'm not vindictive," said Mrs. R. H. Vogan of Peach Orchard, Arkansas, "but the German people must be punished in some way." One high school girl from St. Louis's Central High exclaimed: "I wouldn't treat the Germans that way, even if they aren't human!" And Velma Jones, a black from St. Louis said simply: "I don't know what we're going to do with those people." Most, however, hoped that the showing of such films would prevent future atrocities. "Realizing what these atrocities mean is our only hope for a better life and the end of wars," noted one Coast Guardsman. "I think the films will do some good."[10]

What was in any case particularly striking about Agee's remarks was his inability to face the subject matter of the films, the camps themselves. It remained just propaganda, judged neither true nor false. What Agee might have learned from actually seeing the films was that the cruelties portrayed hit audiences at such a deep level that guilt, shame, and depression were more likely reactions than thirst for revenge.

Agee's review at no time questioned the accuracy of the films, and in that sense it was mild compared with some others. Milton Mayer, writing in *The Progressive,* made the same basic argument against a Carthaginian peace for Germany. "Vengeance will not raise the tortured dead," he concluded. "It will not build a better world than the one that produced the Nazis." But in order to get to that conclusion he felt it necessary to cast doubt on the authenticity of what had been revealed about Nazi atrocities. Mayer began by calling the stories and photographs in the newspapers "unspeakable," and *"almost* unimaginable." He admitted every last one might be true, but whether true or false they seemed aimed at inspiring hate of a prostrate enemy. It was clear that he could not himself believe them:

> Let us assume that the stories are all true. There are, to be sure, fantastic discrepancies in the reports. And the character of the evidence—including photographs of gas chambers and piles of emaciated bodies, the testimony of liberated prisoners, and the inspections of the scene after the fact—would not be held under ordinary American judicial practice to be sufficient for conviction in a capital crime.

Even if all the stories were true, he argued, still these were the crimes of individuals and not a whole people. Justice should be served, not indiscriminate passions of vengeance. Yet in the rest of his long column, he felt the need to continually doubt the reality of the evidence.[11]

This underlying suspicion and outright denial especially enraged the GIs who had witnessed the camps in person. Some attempted to show their own snapshots of what they had seen to others, but all too frequently they were dismissed as fabrications or deemed too disgusting to look at. This sometimes led to a silence among the soldiers about the camps, an extension of that isolation most combat veterans feel about describing war to those who have never experienced battle. In this case, however, even some of their buddies in the service would not accept what they had to say as true. "I took a set of [photographs] back to England and people couldn't believe it," remembered Bert Weston in trying to tell others of Ebensee. "They said it's propaganda. The GIs who went back to Paris had the same experience. . . . They said people didn't believe them."[12]

This same rejection sometimes happened in families. "I told my mother and father about it, and they didn't know what the hell I was talkin' about," recalled Jack Hallett, who saw Dachau. "So it was from that point on I rarely mentioned it except after the kids were old enough to understand it.[13] Philip Carlquist encountered more active resistance: "They were such terrible pictures that, when I got home, my wife destroyed them. She tore them up. She couldn't believe it; she tore them up."[14]

Some persisted, however, even in the face of moral qualms. Joseph Kushlis, who took photographs at Ohrdruf, remembered that he had hesitated about taking the pictures of the victims. "It did occur to me that there was probably a question of morality or decency in even photographing these unfortunate people," he remembered, "but then I quickly resolved the question to my own satisfaction in realizing that here was history that should be recorded." He was glad he had. When he came home, he noticed that it was important to those who saw his pictures that they were not Signal Corps photos. "I think it made up their minds for them if they had any doubt," he observed. "Here was something taken by a strict amateur photographer in which there could be no doctoring of scenes and no faking of film. What I took was there. It was fact."[15]

Another incident confirmed the resistance of many to any sort of second-hand evidence about the camps. General Omar Bradley ordered that Buchenwald be closed to groups seeking first-hand proof of Nazi atrocities. It seemed that necessary sanitary measures, including the removal and burial of the piles of corpses upon which visitors had naturally focused, had removed "any educational value" such tours once possessed. "In fact," he noted, "many feel quite skeptical that previous conditions actually existed." All the press reports, all the photographs and motion pictures, all the confirmation of public officials and publishers meant little to a small number of those who had not seen the bodies themselves, who had not smelled the feces and rotting flesh. The will to deny, it was clear, could sometimes triumph over all but the most direct experience.[16]

The mixed success of the campaign to educate Americans about Nazi atrocities was demonstrated in a Gallup poll taken in early May of 1945, one that indicated progress from the poll taken in November 1944. A cross section of the American public was asked: "What do you think of the reports that the Germans have killed many in concentration camps or let them starve to death— are they true or not true?" Eighty-four percent answered "true"; 9 percent believed the statement to be "true, but exaggerated"; only 4 percent answered "doubtful, hard to believe" or "not true"; 3 percent couldn't decide. Although the press regularly reported figures in the range of three to seven or eight million victims, the median average guess of those responding was one million. The American public believed and now could picture Nazi cruelty, but even so there were those who felt the need to back away from its full dimensions.[17]

The Gallup poll could indicate a strain of reluctance to accept fully that which had been presented, but it could not explain that reluctance. The nature of polling in general, indeed the very structure of such questions and answers, pointed to an explanation in the realm of the rational. Americans were asked what they *thought* about the reportage of Nazi crimes, and to express that thought by telling *how much* they believed. They were even asked to make a quantitative estimate. However, the reasons for a need to qualify hinted at in the poll might best be uncovered in speculation as to how people must have *felt* when forced to confront the graphic evidence of atrocities.

Take the examples of literary critics Alfred Kazin and Susan Sontag, both Jewish and both deeply affected by the revelations of the camps. Kazin described what he actually saw as he viewed the first films from Belsen. "On the screen," he remembered, "sticks in black-and-white prison garb leaned on a wire, staring dreamily at the camera; other sticks shuffled about, or sat vaguely on the ground next to an enormous pile of bodies, piled up like cordwood, from which protruded legs, arms, heads. A few guards were collected sullenly in a corner, and for a moment a British Army bulldozer was shown digging an enormous hole in the ground. Then the sticks would come back on the screen, hanging on the wire, looking at us." Kazin had believed the stories of genocide from the first time he heard them in 1942, but even he had to distance himself in his description of the film. The scenes at Belsen took on a nightmare-like silence, a jumbled anarchy of spliced horrors, with survivors reduced to ghoulish "sticks" that looked out at the viewers. Kazin remembered his feelings as "unbearable," and only by turning the reality of the newsreel into a nightmare could he recount it. As for Susan Sontag, her first exposure to scenes of Belsen and Dachau in photographs caused a similar duality of pain and numbness. "I felt irrevocably grieved, wounded," she wrote, "but a part of my feelings started to tighten; something went dead; something still is crying."[18]

These were the highly self-scrutinized constructions of introspective intellectuals, trained to divine the meaning and structure of their feelings. One can only assume that less self-searching Americans experienced the same deadening, but experienced it as a reluctance to face the deepest reality of what they saw: death itself, death without meaning or ceremony; living human beings stripped of all outward signs of humanity, looking like "sticks" and acting like "animals"; the results of an orgy of violence, the urge toward which resides in us all. In facing the camps Americans faced the profoundest fear and guilt and were forced to view the most barren vision of the end. Why should they not recoil from the evidence of such realities?

8 | Displaced Persons

The image that news makes of reality is ephemeral; the reality itself remains. Piles of dead, sticks staring at the camera, the deep vacant eyes and emaciated body of the survivor multiplied hundreds or thousands of times—these were the fixed images that stunned Americans, and the realities from which they shrank. After the celebrations of V-E Day the public concentrated less on the victims and more on the perpetrators. Survivors remained nameless symbols; the names one heard instead were Irme Grese, the Bitch of Belsen, or Ilse Koch, the Beast of Buchenwald, as Americans clamored to personify evil in the sadism of individuals rather than face its pervasiveness in the system. The Nuremberg trials opened in late 1945; for a while attention turned to the surviving leaders of the Nazi state and the unwieldy apparatus set up to review and punish their crimes. As postwar inflation appeared and the Cold War heated up, even the Nazis seemed pushed from consciousness. In the minds of most Americans, the survivors quickly became shadows of a distant nightmare.

In Europe the survivors were still people, many of them broken in body, mind, and spirit. To be sure, liberation celebrations at every major camp proclaimed a new day, and those survivors healthy enough to cheer fervently affirmed its coming. At Buchenwald, Dachau, Flossenburg, and Mauthausen, anthems were sung and pictures of Roosevelt, Stalin, and Churchill paraded. Yet even as soldier and prisoner alike declared the end of war and captivity, those broken by the camps continued to die and those who celebrated knew that it would take more than a parade to heal wounds and begin life anew.

The days after liberation were trying ones. Each camp was a small anarchy, with little food, bad water, and death and disease rampant. The first mission for medical personnel was to separate the living from the dead and to make every effort to save those who still clung to life. Even this basic task was overwhelming in its scope and demands. For instance, at Mauthausen, where 18,000 prisoners were at the mother camp on May 5 when the 11th Armored Division entered its gates, 700 unburied bodies littered the grounds, two hundred or more inmates were dying each day, and malnutrition, typhus, tuberculosis, and other diseases preyed on those still living. On May 7 two army doctors organized a health program; soon more doctors arrived, and within two weeks the entire staff of the 130th Evacuation Hospital, thirty physicians and forty nurses, had set up shop. Major tasks included the isolating of survivors with communicable diseases, treating various serious infections, and creating a flexible diet regimen with which to rehabilitate inmates in various stages of starvation and malnutrition. Some prisoners had so withered that they could only be fed intravenously; others began with small amounts of easily digested food and slowly worked their way toward a normal diet, while still others could withstand almost normal feedings after only a few days. By the first week of June the death rate had fallen to an average of 5 to 15 per week, and only 1621 survivors remained hospitalized. Medical rehabilitation efforts for other camps enjoyed similar successes.[1]

Once American personnel at the camps looked beyond the simple but crucial question of saving lives, they found themselves to be a part of a dismal circus. From the outside, demands of war crimes investigators, reporters, and dignitaries for organized tours of the camps stretched weeks beyond the first shocking days after liberation. Especially at Buchenwald and Dachau, crowds of visitors circled preserved piles of bodies or paraded through barracks inhabited by the sick and dying, impeding needed medical and sanitary operations. After the first few weeks, ogling at survivors crossed the line between needed reportage and voyeurism. "The remaining prisoners are on show as exhibits," commented an Amer-

Survivors at Buchenwald.

Survivors at Buchenwald.

Survivor quarters at Belsen.

ican officer who visited Buchenwald in early June, "in their rags, and with their physical deformities, etc. The few people we talked to expressed no resentment at this, but it is felt that, even so, this is quite an unjustifiable prostitution of their misfortunes."[2]

The liberated prisoners themselves also bewildered innocent American onlookers. Despite what they knew about what their wards had undergone, some Americans never ceased to wonder why, even after food had been made readily abundant, the survivors pushed and shoved their way to the soup kettle or bread basket. Others were appalled to find some indifferent to nudity or personal cleanliness. Nor was it readily understood why many were slow to volunteer for work, even though it might help the condition of the camp.[3]

Survivors in somewhat better health, whose personal habits approximated normality, disappointed in other ways. Naïve Americans who thought that the camp experience might bring a certain unity and spirit of tolerance were puzzled to find that it seemed to have bred quite opposite traits. Though survivors all, Germans still looked down upon Russians and Poles; Poles still hated the Jews; and everyone seemed to despise Gypsies. In a striking example of such strife, Americans at Dachau were dumbfounded by a number of Polish survivors who threatened to riot if a public Jewish service were held on the main parade ground. The onetime prisoners clustered in national and religious groups and complained, often justly, about unequal treatment. The prisoner committees that helped run the liberated camps worked strenuously to reduce such friction, though they themselves sometimes indulged in petty arguments and discriminations.[4]

In the end, most Americans at the camps in the weeks after liberation came away with a sobered but not unsympathetic view of the survivors. They learned that imprisonment and slave labor bred few heroes and martyrs and strengthened few virtues, that it encouraged a survivalist ethic that left a lasting imprint. It was with genuine happiness for the prisoners and genuine relief for themselves, then, that they cheered and even shed tears as busloads and truckloads and parades of camp inmates headed for home to make a new life.

Most did get home, but a significant number did not. While Western Europeans in reasonable physical condition had no trouble returning to their native lands, for Eastern Europeans and especially Eastern European Jews it was not so simple. Many Poles did not wish to return to a Poland under the new Communist regime. Numerous Russians, though in theory required to return to the Soviet Union by Allied treaty obligations, avoided repatriation in various ways. Finally Polish, Hungarian, and other Eastern European Jews, fearing with good reason that anti-Semitism would continue to be a powerful force in their homelands, hoped to gain entry to Palestine, the United States, or some other friendly nation.[5]

The fate of these hundreds of thousands of "unrepatriable" survivors of the camps was decided in the whirlwind of postwar

French displaced persons heading home.

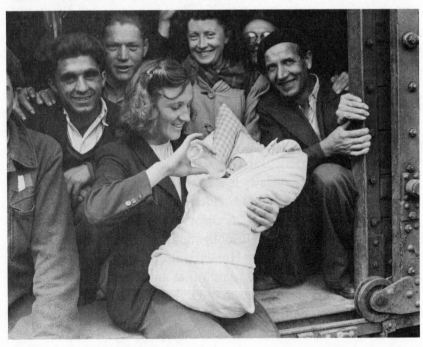

Returning French displaced persons.

Europe, where as many as thirty million persons found themselves away from home at the end of the war and where Cold War considerations had begun to affect every political and social decision. Allied governments that had been shocked just weeks and months before by the horrors of Dachau, Buchenwald, and Belsen, now lumped the most needful of camp survivors side-by-side with vast millions of others and called them all displaced persons, or DPs.

The displaced persons made strange bedfellows. There were of course Jews, Gypsies, political prisoners, and persons of the conquered nations who had been brought to Germany for slave labor or eventual extermination. Then there were those from the Baltic countries who had come voluntarily to work in wartime Germany, whether for economic reasons or pro-Nazi sympathies or both. Anti-Soviet Russians who volunteered to fight under the Nazi military umbrella also sought refuge far from their homeland. In addition, millions of ethnic Germans from beyond Germany's eastern borders and Germans from within them fled the advance of the Soviet Army and hoped for better treatment in the British, French, and American occupation zones. By the middle of 1945, the DP population had swelled further as surviving Jews in the East began to flee new outbreaks of native anti-Semitism and as the Eastern European countries themselves began to deport ethnic Germans who had lived within their borders.[6]

The Allies had anticipated that displaced persons would be a problem in the postwar world and had started making plans for dealing with the situation as early as 1942. In 1943 they created UNRRA (United Nations Relief and Rehabilitation Administration) to oversee distribution of food, clothing, medicine, and other care to the needy. These plans were later augmented as the magnitude of the task became apparent, but few anticipated the enormous numbers that presented themselves in the summer of 1945. Of the thirty million displaced persons in Europe, about 7.5 to 9 million were in the Western zones of occupied Germany, Austria, and Italy alone. While 6 million of these were miraculously repatriated by the end of 1945, that still left 1.5 to 2 million displaced persons under the direct control of the occupying armies. There were too few UNRRA workers to aid Allied military personnel, too few

Jewish child prisoners from Buchenwald board transport to go to France, Palestine, and the United States, June 1945.

Child prisoners await trip to a new life in Switzerland.

places to house the refugees, and little clear sense of what eventually would or should happen to them. Plans that had meant to create a humane finale to the war ended up, at least for the unrepatriables, as a dismal holding action with little in the way of direction or resources.[7]

Numbers were not the only problem. Plans for treatment of displaced persons were drawn up along lines of nationality, with little or no notice taken of unique individual or group situations. Thus citizens of Nazi-occupied nations were to receive the full benefits of DP programs, while Austrian, German, Hungarian, and Italian displaced persons were basically defined as "the enemy." The policy made some sense on paper, but in practice it was a moral disaster. It made those Yugoslavs, Ukrainians, Russians, Latvians, Lithuanians, and Estonians who had volunteered for service with the Nazis favored refugees, while it placed German, Austrian, and Hungarian Jews and political "persecutees" in an unclear category that, depending on who was making the decision, put them under the care of UNRRA or made them the responsibility of their own country, with few or none of the benefits that were available to other DPs.[8]

Another unfortunate abstraction was the Allied policy of not recognizing religious differences. Again, though a noble sentiment on paper, it failed to recognize that Jewish displaced persons were far more in need of help than most others. One statistic perhaps shows the state of the Jewish survivors better than any other. Of the 60,000 Jews in camps at the time of liberation, twenty thousand died within a week. Those who lived were usually alone in the world, in a terrible state of psychological and physical trauma, in dire need of care, understanding, and patience. What happened in fact was that they were thrown together in assembly centers with the Balts, Poles, and other healthier displaced persons, many of whom were anti-Semites and a great number of whom were actually Nazi collaborators. Some of the Balts and Hungarians had been functionaries and guards at the concentration camps.[9]

Worse still, in general those who had voluntarily gone to Germany during the war came to be viewed as the elite of the displaced persons, while the Jews and others deemed inferior by the

Nazis were often seen as bothersome rabble. The reasons for this situation were varied and many. The Balts presented themselves to the occupying forces as polite, clean, and ready to please. They had suffered deprivations during the war, but hardly the sort of treatment common in the concentration camps. Most had lived in German workers' quarters or with farm families; others had actually served in the army or the SS. Some had even applied for German citizenship before the end of the war. Thus while they were certainly something of a disadvantaged group in May 1945, most had retained their basic social skills. They also generally got along well with local German civilians, something to be expected from old allies. Furthermore, the political realities of the nascent Cold War made it easy for some Americans to forget the Balts' Nazi connections and to see them in a new light—as refugees from Communism. In short, the chaos of postwar Europe and the growing sense of the Soviet Union as the new enemy made well-behaved, healthy Balts a DP administrator's dream.[10]

The Jews were another story. The camps had taken their toll, and when survivors were herded into their new quarters in old army barracks and the like, they had not yet recovered from past physical and mental trauma. U.S. Army inspectors found that the Jews could not keep their camps in order—kitchens were filthy, living quarters were overcrowded and in shambles, and human excrement littered hallways and cooking areas. Nor to the average American on the scene did they appear overly virtuous. The Jews seemed distrustful of just about everyone, avoided work, and seemed interested only in what they could procure in the way of food and clothing. Old anti-Semitic stereotypes blended with these scenes of degradation to leave a rather unfavorable impression on many in the occupation force. Especially for those Americans who had not seen the concentration camps, such behavior appeared to be more innate than situational, and in any case indicative of relative inferiority in comparison with the Balts.[11]

Even more striking was American occupation force behavior toward the DPs when compared with their relations with German civilians. One need only imagine the situation at a DP camp like Landsberg, in Bavaria, where until late in 1945 the basically Jew-

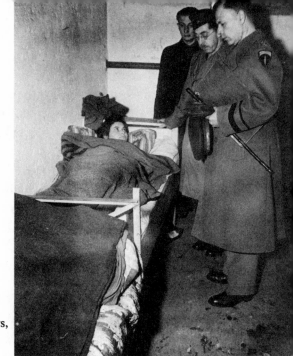

General W. Bedell Smith and USFET adviser on Jewish affairs, Judge Simon Rifkind, inspect Landsberg living quarters.

General W. Bedell Smith and Judge Simon Rifkind inspect lavatories at Landsberg DP camp.

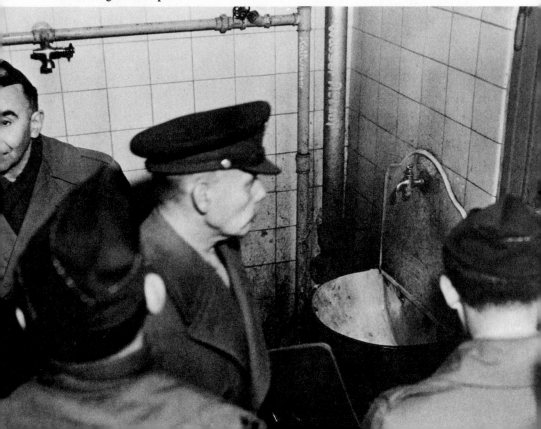

ish population was kept behind barbed wire and passes were required to travel in and out of the camp, while the Germans outside the camp were free to come and go as they liked. Somehow the martyrs of the camps had been put in quarantine, while the enemy had been made free.

Several forces combined to create this turnabout. First, despite the fears of James Agee, Milton Mayer, and many others, the American occupation of Germany was extraordinarily benign. This was in part because of the fear that a harsh peace might reproduce the very conditions that brought Hitler to power, and in part because it was clear that Germany would figure mightily in the expected future struggle with the Soviet Union. In a matter of months our enemy had become our ally.

At the same time, even before such general policy directions had become clear, a strange chemistry had begun to work between American soldiers, most of whom had never fired a shot at the Nazis, and German civilians. The title of an article published in March 1946 put it bluntly: "Why So Many GIs Like the Germans Best." Authors Richard Joseph and Waverly Root attempted to explain a phenomenon that Joseph noticed upon returning to the States after the war. He was asked to sign a Red Cross register, one that had a column for the returning soldier to list his favorite European country. He perused the register and calculated that roughly four out of five soldiers preferred Germany. This confirmed a sense that he had already gotten in Europe. GIs complained about the French and about the English, but one rarely heard complaints about the Germans. The few who did curse them, he noted, "were combat men who had seen their friends die in battle, who had viewed the bodies of Americans shot after surrendering, who had smelled the corpses of Buchenwald or Dachau." As for those who came after them, they only knew the old enemy "as peaceful, artfully friendly hosts."[12]

The reasons were not hard to find. Though German cities had been heavily damaged, many of the areas where American troops were stationed remained quaint villages with well-fed, polite citizens and, by reputation at least, very willing women. To the lonely GI, German towns looked and felt more like hometown

America than anywhere else in Europe. The German wooing of the American was so successful, in fact, that "many an American soldier carried his defense of the Germans to the point of accusing the American authorities of having invented the atrocity stories."[13]

Perceptive American officers also began to notice this disturbing phenomenon, especially as it affected treatment of displaced persons. In July 1945, Captain C. E. Jack felt moved to issue a memorandum entitled "DPS VS. GERMAN AUTHORITIES," in which he outlined the ways in which German community leaders undercut rehabilitation efforts and sympathy for the displaced persons. Basically the problem was that with the peace, requisitioning of supplies for displaced persons changed from direct confiscations from local enemy populations to more complicated bureaucratic requests under the terms of the occupation. As Jack delineated the problem, he revealed the various ways in which the Military Government personnel often allowed unfair practices to be instituted against the DPs by the local Germans as a result of conscious or unconscious comparison of the two populations.[14]

First, Captain Jack pointed out that appearance alone biased the GIs against the DPs. DPs lived in barracks, barns, schoolhouses, and used common sanitary facilities. A DP had only a few pieces of clothing beyond what he wore on his back, sometimes resorted to petty theft, and displayed a highly defensive attitude toward authority. "He has learned to distrust promises and pieces of paper," Jack wrote. "His world revolves around food and shelter. In American slang, he looks and acts like a bum." By contrast, the Germans were well dressed, better fed, lived at home with family, and addressed an American officer with respect. This simple contrast often made the Military Government officer believe the stories and complaints of Germans and discount those of the DPs.

Language difficulties only compounded problems for the DP. While German interpreters were usually available, those who spoke Polish, Russian, Serbo-Croatian, or other DP languages were rare. "Quite often the interpreting is done by a German civilian," Jack reported, "which naturally does not help a DP's plea against the Germans. In any case, the misunderstandings resulting from language differences are numerous and certainly not amusing to the DP when it makes the difference between eating and not eating."

Finally Jack contrasted a common problem—giving general orders to locals but allowing them to drag their feet for lack of specific instructions or follow up—with examples of proper supervision and enforcement of orders. The cases were instructive. At Linz, for instance, Jack requested that the Military Government order civil officials to provide 5000 men's suits and 5000 pairs of shoes for DPs at Mauthausen. The Austrians put on a volunteer collection, which after three days netted a thousand each of pairs of shoes and suits. The balance was due five days later. When Jack returned, the Austrians informed him that logistical problems allowed them to collect only two truckloads more. When he asked the Austrians why he hadn't been informed beforehand so things might be cleared up, he received a "shrug of the shoulders." Jack immediately ordered them to fill out their load from clothing stores in Linz. It was an order that was quickly obeyed.

Jack ended his report with a sobering observation. While he noted that the Germans certainly suffered during the war, "comparatively few Germans were snatched out of their homes and forced into labor, torture and death in foreign countries." Which was precisely what the Germans did to peoples like the Poles. "To a typical German," he continued, "the Poles are sub-average people. . . . They still view them as a 'barracks' race. If they are sub-average, it is because the Germans made them that way. Yet I cannot recall how many times I have heard MG officers say 'These damn Poles—it's small wonder why the Germans treated them as they did.' This statement to me is the most discouraging thing in DP work, because it reflects the thinking of a considerable number of Americans."

Leadership at the top might have thrown some weight to the side of the DPs. Indeed, as Leonard Dinnerstein has noted, those displaced persons located, for instance, in the Seventh Army area in Germany, lived with some measure of human respect. Not so in much of Bavaria, where General George S. Patton presided over the occupation. From the beginning Patton, more concerned with rebuilding Germany to face the Russian threat than being fair to displaced persons or true to de-Nazification, gained a reputation for placing in power civilian authorities who either had Nazi records or had evinced scant devotion to democratic ideals. As for the displaced persons, Patton saw their very existence as a misfortune. The same man who had sickened at the sight of Ohrdruf now made invidious distinctions between the DPs based on their condition. He singled out "the Jewish type of DP" as "a sub-human species without any of the cultural or social refinements of our time."[15]

In Patton's case, what had been a garden-variety genteel anti-Semitism before and during the war became a rabid, paranoid rage. The Jews, he thought, were out to get him and his good sense policies in Germany. He opposed the war crimes trials, calling them "not cricket" and "semitic." He blamed hostile press reactions to GI fraternization with the Germans on vengeful Jews. He saw the "Semitic influence in the press" as trying to "implement Communism" and making sure that "all business men of German ancestry and non-Jewish antecedents [were] thrown out of their jobs."[16]

This was the man who, until he was relieved of his duties in the fall of 1945, in part because of such attitudes, was in charge of the single largest concentration of Jewish DPs. Not surprisingly, he usually put the worst construction on their appalling condition. When General Louis Craig told him about the awful things he saw in one camp and speculated that the persons in the camp either never had any sense of decency or lost it in the concentration camps, Patton was sure that "no people could have sunk to the level of degradation these have reached in the short space of four years." Once Patton talked to an UNRRA worker who, when the General noted that Estonian DPs (Balts who had moved to Germany voluntarily during the war) cut wood at four times the rate of the Jews, pointed out that most of the Jewish DPs suffered from a camp-induced psychopathic condition that would improve. Patton found this argument unconvincing. "I have never looked at a group who seem to be more lacking in intelligence and spirit," he wrote in his diary. "Practically all of them had the flat brownish gray eye common among the Hawaiians which, to my mind, indicates very low intelligence." Once Eisenhower cajoled him into attending

Jewish Shavuot services held for released prisoners at Buchenwald, May 1945.

Yom Kippur services at a Jewish camp. ". . . [T]he smell was so terrible," he confided in his diary, "that I almost fainted and actually about three hours later lost my lunch as the result of remembering it."[17]

One did not need to be particularly anti-Semitic or anti-Polish or even friendly to the Germans to find the DPs annoying and sometimes exasperating. One only had to be an American occupation officer trying to keep law and order. To the bureaucratic and task-oriented Military Government, which made little room for considerations of recent history and most of all saw its task as creating a smoothly run occupation, unruliness and lawbreaking were serious offenses no matter the persons or reasons. To the honest if naïve keeper of the peace, an incident that occurred in Bavaria in April 1946 must have seemed well-nigh unexplainable except as proof of DP unfitness for freedom. A rumor had spread that two Jewish DP guards had been kidnapped from their school at Diessen. The official Army intelligence memo read:

> . . . This report was started by another DP at the school, who had gone to the post and found that they were not there. Immediately after that about 50 inmates of the camp there were reported to have gone wild, stopping Germans and asking for their identity, and beating up some of them. It seems that the information about the kidnapping spread to the LANDSBERG camp, but there the story was spread that DP children had been kidnapped. That was about 0930, and immediately thereafter the DPs of this camp stopped a German bus, stabbed the bus driver and overturned the bus, which burned. No casualties other than the bus driver are reported. However, it is reported that there are now 6 Germans in the hospital as a result of the riot, 12 more having been admitted, treated and discharged.[18]

Few American officers understood the pent-up fears and anger and dark memories that caused this sort of hysteria, and most tended to see in every such disruption one more proof of the disreputable nature of the DP population. Even if the Americans could sympathize, the actions of the DPs were at odds with the goals of American policy.

At times the results of such a clash of sympathy and policy could be heartbreaking. In September 1945 a trainload of six hundred or so Polish Jews attempted to enter the American zone in Germany from the Czech border. They had left Poland as signs of renewed anti-Semitism began to appear, and felt that their best hope of survival was to enter a DP camp and wait for possible emigration to Palestine, the United States, or some other non-European haven. At the Pilsen reception camp they attempted to masquerade as German Jews returning to Munich, but their "faulty" German accents revealed them as imposters. Since those in command of the displaced persons felt that the camps had already become overcrowded and that the flow of Jewish and other refugees had to be stopped, they ordered that no further refugees be accepted in the Bavarian sector. Thus, after a few days stay at Camp Karlov awaiting a train to send them back, the Jews were loaded on a train headed to the East.

At that point all the collective memory of Nazi brutality came into play. The American soldiers saw themselves as simply returning illegal refugees to Prague, where they would be dealt with as the Czech government saw fit. The survivors saw themselves as being sent back to Poland and to their death, reimagining what had already happened to them once under the Nazis and what seemed to be happening again even after the war. They resisted the repatriation in whatever way they could. Pat Frank, a reporter for the Overseas News Agency and the *New York Post,* interviewed American personnel involved. "My job was sickening," declared a Jewish private from Chicago who helped load the refugees on trucks destined for the railroad station. "Men threw themselves on their knees in front of me, tore open their shirts, and screamed, 'Kill me now!' They would say 'You might just as well kill me now. I am dead anyway if I go back to Poland.' They kept jumping off the trucks. And we had to use force."[19]

Luba Zindel of Cracow, who had been able to stay because she was having a baby when the train left, told her story to the reporter. She and her husband had been in a camp near Lublin for three years, until the Russians liberated them in 1944. They returned to Cracow and had begun to pick up the pieces of their life. On the first Sabbath of August 1945, the synagogue they were attending was attacked by uniformed members of General Anders's army, a nationalist and anti-Semitic group that fought both the Nazis and the Communists. "They were shouting that we had committed ritual murders," Zindel told Pat Frank. "They began firing at us and beating us up. My husband was sitting beside me. He fell down, his face full of bullets." She saw no alternative but to escape to the West.[20]

The story was reported under headlines such as the *New York Post*'s "Patton Turned Back 600 Jews Fleeing Terror in Poland," and the Army felt a rebuttal was necessary. It pointed out that the refugees, after all, attempted to enter Germany illegally, were treated humanely while awaiting repatriation, but had to be sent back to Czechoslovakia. The memorandum emphasized that they were being sent to *Prague* not to Poland, and that reports from that city said that they had been settled in a Czechoslovak camp. The displaced persons camps had been deemed too crowded, emigration from the East had been stopped, and the return of these refugees simply carried out the orders then in effect.[21]

The state of relations between the occupation forces and the displaced persons upset a good many Americans, and pressure soon began to be exerted by Jewish groups and other interested parties to improve conditions. Reports about the DP camps were so abysmal that President Truman sent Earl Harrison, a member of the State Department, to make a personal inspection and appraisal of conditions, especially those prevailing in camps with populations made up predominantly of Jewish survivors of the concentration camps. Harrison and his committee toured the camps in July 1945 and issued their report in August. The main body of the report began with a simple and chastening statement:

> Generally speaking, three months after V-E Day and even longer after the liberation of individual groups, many Jewish displaced persons and other possibly non-repatriables are living under guard behind barbed-wire fences, in camps of several descriptions, (built by the Germans for slave-laborers and Jews) including some of the most notorious of the concentration camps, amidst crowded, frequently unsanitary and generally grim conditions, in complete idleness, with no opportunity, except surreptitiously, to communicate with the outside world, waiting, hoping for some word of encouragement and action in their behalf.[22]

Harrison did note that the health of the survivors had improved dramatically and some attempts had been made to secure decent clothing and a reasonable and consistent diet. Still there was room for much improvement in the clothing, sanitary, living, and dietary arrangements provided for these broken men and women. "Beyond knowing that they are no longer in danger of the gas chambers, torture, and other forms of violent death," Harrison wrote, "they see—and there is—little change." All of this was only underlined when, "as in so many cases, they [were] able to look from their crowded and bare quarters and see the German civilian population, particularly in the rural areas, to all appearances living normal lives in their own homes."[23]

Harrison argued that in the case of the Jews, the first and

most important thing to do was to recognize them as a group with special needs and identity. Particular attention should be paid, Harrison added, to resettling the Jews where they wished and where they would not be persecuted. That meant Palestine and, if that was not possible, the United States, colonies of the British Empire, or countries in South America should be encouraged to accept them.[24]

Harrison's solution to the Jewish DP problem, then, centered on expediting emigration, especially to Palestine, and improving temporary camp conditions. He recommended a general approach based on the experience of a few commanders in the field who had favored, when necessary, the displaced persons at the expense of the local German population. In these isolated instances, German houses were turned over to survivors, food and clothing forcibly requisitioned, and in other ways both material and psychological the displaced persons were made to feel they were on the winning side of the war. Harrison also recommended that military administration be terminated, and that a much strengthened UNRRA take over operations. Finally, he suggested freer access for the DPs in and out of camp and the elimination of barbed wire and other reminders of the concentration camps. Most of all, he urged that, while awaiting emigration, separate camps be set up for Jewish DPs.[25]

The report ended on a conciliatory note, one which comprehended as many had not the enormous task involved in helping the displaced persons. Harrison called the repatriation effort "a phenomenal performance." Further, he noted that there were numerous exceptions to every criticism he made. A general had predicted that he would find among the camps "some that are quite good, some that are very bad, with the average something under satisfactory." His trip "confirmed that prediction in all respects." Having done such a fine job with the repatriables, it was time to improve the lot of those whose problems were more complex. "The civilized world," he emphasized, "owes it to this handful of survivors to provide them with a home where they can again settle down and begin to live as human beings."[26]

The Harrison Report sparked a striking attempt on the part of President Truman and General Eisenhower to improve conditions. It spurred further pressures from Washington on London to open up immigration quotas to Palestine. And at the displaced persons camps changes began to be made, both in the details of everyday life and in the separation of Jews from other DPs. Those in Washington thought of additional ways to ameliorate the condition of displaced persons, Jews and non-Jews alike. The War Department initiated a campaign of education for the occupation troops, one that aimed at reminding them of what the DPs had suffered. A typical publication, an "Army Talk" on DPs used in enlisted men's discussion groups, recounted the sordid history of Nazi cruelties and emphasized that the displaced persons were the product of that history. It explained that the DPs lived in "an unfriendly and alien country," and could not be expected to be very enthusiastic about rebuilding a Germany that destroyed their lives. The publication concluded by urging "tolerance, patience, kindness" and stressed the "moral obligation" Americans had to give the DPs "the chance to regain their health, their strength, their confidence in the future . . . ."[27]

However, the fact remained that nothing was easy in the world of the displaced persons, as the experience of sympathetic American officers demonstrated. In the wake of the Harrison Report, Major Irving Heymont was given command of the districts that included Landsberg Displaced Persons Camp. At the time of Heymont's coming, Landsberg was one of the larger and one of the shoddier camps. It housed 6000 DPs, 5000 of whom were Jews and the rest Hungarians and a variety of Balts. The quarters themselves were once German army barracks, but had fallen on hard times since too many DPs were forced into buildings meant for reasonably comfortable garrison life. "The camp is filthy beyond description," Heymont wrote in his first letter home. "Sanitation is virtually unknown. Words fail me when I try to think of an adequate description." The mood of the DPs was more depressing still. "With a few exceptions," Heymont lamented, "the people of the camp themselves appear demoralized beyond hope of rehabilitation. They appear to be beaten both spiritually and physically, with no hopes or incentives for the future."[28]

Heymont's plan was to enlist actively the residents' aid in cleaning up the camp. He met with the camp committee, assured them full cooperation if they could motivate the survivors to pitch

163

in, and enlisted the aid of Jewish-American soldiers in the area. These efforts began to pay off almost immediately. He also ordered the barbed wire torn down, freer access to town given to the DPs, and heavy guards removed. Nonetheless the road was rocky, and after initial improvement the dirt began to pile up again. Heymont began to see that the damage done to the survivors in the camps would not easily be undone. Then, on October 4, he was jolted into recognition of the deepest emotions running through the camp. It had been decided that overcrowding was one of the basic problems at Landsberg, and that to alleviate the condition nearby German housing would be requisitioned. When word got to the DPs, they gathered to watch the Germans being evicted, but soon got upset because the Germans were taking with them household items that the DPs needed. It was not long before the survivors were forcing their way into the houses as they were being vacated, and "looting and pillaging." Rumors swept through the German community, including one that the Jews were going to take over the town with American blessing. The tables had been turned so to speak but, as the survivors pointed out, not quite. "The Germans were not being led off to death or torture camps," Heymont was reminded. "They were being allowed to take everything but their furniture. Their families were not being broken up." This argument had its impact. Later when Germans complained of the looting and requested their property, Heymont noted that "they were not being dragged off to a concentration camp with only the clothing on their backs and that they [were] not going to see their families starved or gassed or otherwise killed."[29]

Heymont's sympathy for the DPs increased day by day. He was particularly incensed by American military government authorities who blamed the existence of a black market on the DPs, one that operated in all parts of Germany and was engaged in by Germans, Allied military personnel, and DPs alike. Yet one Landsberg-based American official was so "phobic" about the problem that he stopped Jews in the streets and roughed them up, always claiming that he was hunting black marketeers. Heymont did not deny the participation of camp dwellers, but recognized that they were small operators in comparison with those in the German population at-large and in the Allied military. He was further angered by the extreme sentences sometimes handed out to DPs for infractions ignored when committed by others. One DP was given three months in jail for having several pounds of butter in his possession. Another was given a similar sentence for bartering army shirts for cigarettes. Meanwhile, GIs quite openly traded cigarettes and other valuables with German civilians with little fear of punishment.[30]

Heymont turned the camp over to civilian authorities in the beginning of December 1945, but not before he had initiated changes that would slowly make life more bearable. As for himself, he had grown considerably. "[T]here is no doubt in my mind that the few months I spent at Landsberg," he wrote 36 years later, "had a greater impact on my outlook on life" than both a long army career and a second career in business. Most of all, it led him to reembrace his once fading sense of Jewishness.[31]

Howard Margol, another Jewish GI, had his own fascinating experience as he helped move Jewish DPs in Austria to better quarters. At one point he was ordered to take a group to an exclusive resort, and was surprised when the rabbi attached to his unit objected. The rabbi was afraid that the DPs, given their condition, would be an embarrassment to other Jews and would only confirm in the minds of the Austrians their traditional anti-Semitism. "It would justify, you know, what they said," recalled Margol: "They were animals, so treat them like animals." Nonetheless General Mark Clark confirmed the orders and the move was carried out. According to Margol, the rabbi's fears were borne out. "They may have been sitting at a table with a white tablecloth, napkins, and everything," he said, "—because these were some of the finest resort hotels in Europe prior to the war, you see, so they had all the fancy crystal and china—but they still sat there and gulped the food down with their hands. They didn't bother to use the silverware or anything. When they had to go to the bathroom, they didn't bother to use the bathroom . . . you know, they had to do whatever they had to do in the hallway, in the grand ballroom, or just wherever they happened to be."[32]

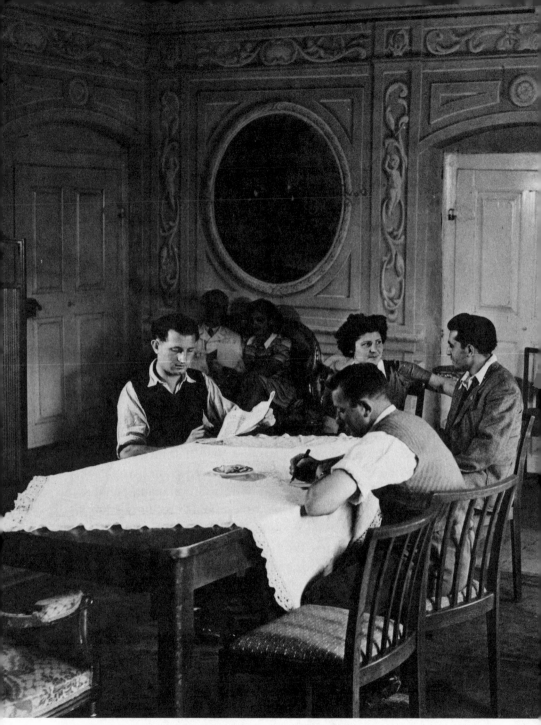

Idealized scene of Jewish DPs at Schloss Duttenstein.

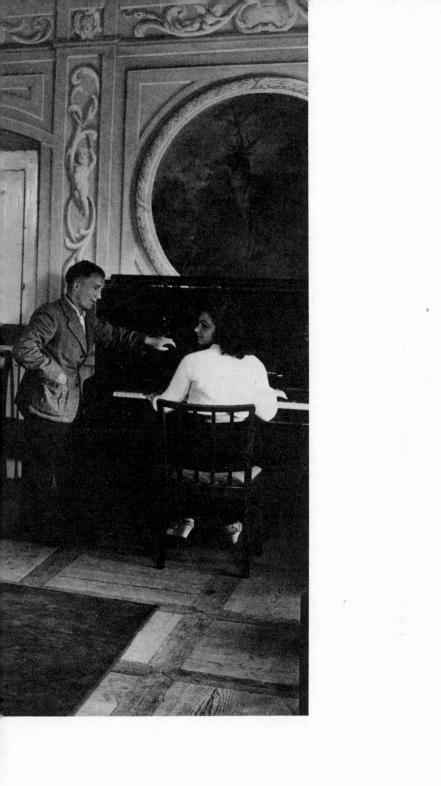

While taking another group of Jewish DPs to a displaced persons camp, however, Margol experienced a demonstration of faith that in many ways transcended his embarrassment at the resort. The move occurred on a Friday, and at sundown the Jews started to raise a commotion:

> We all stopped the trucks to find out what in the world was going on. They all got out of the trucks and sat down in a field alongside the road and said it was Shabbos. This was Friday night and the sun had just gone down. Of course, this was in the Austrian mountains there and the sun went down a little early if anything. They said that they were not going anywhere until the sun went down Saturday night. So I went to some of them and I said, "Look, I'm Jewish; I know what you're talking about, but it's only another 20 to 25 minutes and we'll be at the hotel— and with everything you've been through, what's the big deal . . . so it's another 20 or 24 minutes, you know. You can't stay out here all night in the fields, because the nights get pretty cold in the mountains." But they said they weren't going anywhere and the result is they just laid down in the fields. Of course, we went into town and came back and brought back blankets for them and set up food kitchens and fed them that night and all the next day—and when the sun went down Saturday night, they loaded back in the trucks and went the rest of the way. And so, I say that had a tremendous impact on me.

Jew or Christian, at the concentration camps or at the DP camps, the distance created by fear and strangeness was sometimes broken between liberator and liberated. When that happened mythic victims, hanging on the wire, or annoying DPs, untrustworthy and lazy, became real human beings. When that sense of human connection was broached, the tragedy of the Holocaust only deepened. For the American who came to see the victim of Nazism as a human being much like himself could better count the ways, one by one, in which everything of value and meaning in life could be stripped away and destroyed. That American could better gauge the fragility of life in a world whose possibility for evil had been irrevocably widened.

Epilogue

By the end of 1945 most of the American liberators were back in the United States. As a group, they had little in common besides the fact that they were World War II vets who had seen a concentration camp. Howard Margol re-entered the business world. Bert Weston eventually became a manufacturer's representative for a men's apparel firm. Bill Allison continued his engineering career, while Joseph Kushlis got back into industrial advertising. Fred Mercer became a barber; George King stayed in the army, and later became an academic adviser at University of Miami; Jack Hallett stayed in the service as well, and then worked for the CIA. Philip Carlquist finished his training as a bacteriologist, Samuel Glasshow established a dental practice, and C. W. Doughty became supervisor of customer service for an electrical company. The others made their way into equally diverse positions in society.

Nor had seeing the camps given the liberators a common vision of public or moral issues. Some voted Democratic, some Republican. Some favored our involvement in Vietnam, others opposed the war. All agreed on the need for civil rights for minorities, but each had his own version of what was enough and what was too much. They were of all the major religions and sects and some professed no religion at all. Most, however, did seem to share a revulsion for human cruelty and a vigilance and fear concerning the rise of totalitarianism and political violence. Many associated their experience at the camps with these feelings.

When the liberators came home they did try to tell people

about the camps, but, most ended up responding to the disbelief, disgust, or silence of others with silence of their own. Only a few like Joseph Kushlis made a point of speaking to groups and showing motion pictures of the camps. Some had nightmares about their experiences, most did not. Sometimes at veterans' reunions the memories did come back, but even on these occasions the talk rarely turned to the camps. Old comrades preferred to remember happier moments or smaller, more personal tragedies. Only as they got older and looked back upon the important events of their lives did the encounter with the concentration camps begin to loom large. For their own children and for the world in general, many of the liberators thought it important finally to set down their experiences.

As for the liberated prisoners, they have struggled back to live reborn lives in their homelands or in countries across the globe that accepted them: the United States, Israel, Britain, France, and a score of smaller nations in Europe, Africa, and Latin America. Most have blended in quietly with their surroundings, starting new families and careers and locking dark memories within. A few have sought to keep the camps before the world's conscience. Elie Wiesel, freed at Buchenwald, has made his life a testimony to the survivor's will to live and need to remember. Tadeusz Borowski, liberated at Dachau, wrote a nightmarish account of Auschwitz; some years later he killed himself with gas. Simon Wiesenthal, saved by the Americans at Mauthausen, has spent his life hunting Nazi war criminals. Viktor Frankl, freed at a subcamp of Dachau, has tried to bring meaning to people's lives with a form of psychotherapy he thought through at Auschwitz. More and more, others are beginning to share their stories as the fear increases that the world will forget and ultimately deny what happened at the camps.

The fears are not without foundation, for if the liberations put an end to one double vision, they fostered another. While the photographs, newsreels, and eyewitness accounts of the camps provided a reality that previously lay beyond the imaginations of those attempting to grapple with wartime reports of Nazi genocide, they presented scenes so unbearable that most who viewed them were at once gripped and repulsed by their uncompromising horror. Like the soldiers at the camps, those who came upon Belsen and Buchenwald in a newsreel or picture magazine experienced a potent mixture of shock, anger, shame, guilt, and fear. And like the soldiers, they felt a great need for distance and disconnection.

The immediate impact of the liberations on public opinion displayed these wide and sometimes seemingly contradictory feelings. Shock and anger over the camps certainly galvanized public support for war crimes trials; but having constantly to confront the awful evidence may also have helped to bring about the dramatic wane in concern over war crimes prosecutions that began to appear as the trial of major war criminals at Nuremberg dragged on. There can be no question that sympathy for Nazism's Jewish victims added significantly to American support for the founding of Israel. At the same time, the contemplation of the very same victims, frozen by the camera in their wretched condition at the time of liberation, contributed powerful if only rarely articulated opposition to liberalized immigration quotas that would have allowed many more displaced persons access to the United States.

Over the last forty years the liberations have remained in the public mind largely through a handful of photographs and newsreel excerpts. The scenes portrayed—a pile of bodies at Dachau, a barracks in the Little Camp of Buchenwald, hundreds of corpses laid out in rows before the ruins of buildings at Nordhausen, and among others, bulldozers filling mass graves at Belsen—have attained almost mythic status in a world more and more used to seeing violence every day in full color, live or on videotape, from every corner of the world. It is as if in the spring of 1945 the world lost a certain innocence, and the pictorial remains of that passage have become the *leitmotivs* for our reactions to all that we are presented. We see pictures of Biafra, Bangladesh, Vietnam, or even the freak catastrophe of Jonestown, but what we feel was learned by facing the camps.

But what do we feel? In many ways we undergo the struggle familiar to GIs and wage an inner war between feelings of anger and compassion and the need to run away from the guilt, shame, and fear provoked by viewing atrocity. We, of course, face an image while the soldiers faced a raw reality. No matter how shocked or numbed, the individual soldier could do something to symbolize his feelings, whether that meant a simple act of sharing food or clothing or engaging in revenge. We sit helpless before an image, upset as much by that helplessness as by what we see. Indeed, the photograph itself may make us angry, presenting us with a scene that tears at our insides but about which we can do nothing. By the same token, the GI could not really escape the reality before him. He might invoke every inner defense, but it remained just a defense against an overwhelming environment that he could not escape, one that might haunt him forever. We can put down the picture, choose not to see the movie, turn off the television. That happened in 1945 and since, and in more cases than James Agee's refusal to watch the newsreels. In fact, as the first films of the liberated camps were shown, many people walked out of theaters all over England rather than witness the horrors of the camps. At one cinema in London's Leicester Square and apparently at others in smaller towns and cities, British and other Allied soldiers blocked the exits and told the fleeing patrons to return to their seats. The soldiers wished them to see "what other people had to endure," to "go back and face it."[1]

This blatant conflict between facing the truth and avoiding it has been replaced in our own time by a largely interior drama. We have achieved more sophistication than those English cinema patrons. Our culture has made scenes of the liberation and other evidence of what we now call the Holocaust into universal symbols of humankind's inhuman capacities. They could not be more appropriate. Yet the danger inherent in symbolizing "man's inhumanity to man" with the dead and dying of Buchenwald or of some latter-day tragedy is that it helps us to distance ourselves from both the specific victims and from the fact that each act of genocide or other mass murder or starvation has had its roots in very specific political, economic, and cultural conditions. Raising the vivid documents of atrocity to the level of a general statement on human evil runs the risk of making the sense of helplessness we already feel in the face of such scenes an active truth.

There are no easy answers to how we should deal with our

post-liberation knowledge, for in the end we confront the mutually exclusive desires to remember and to forget. However, we should recognize there are no soldiers to push us back into the theater to face the facts. We must be our own soldiers, constantly on the look out for subtle evasion. We must recognize that if we feel helpless when facing the record of human depravity, there was always a point at which any particular scene of madness could have been stopped.

Acknowledgments

First and foremost I wish to acknowledge my debt to the late Professor Fred J. Crawford of Emory University, to whom this book is dedicated and whose pioneering work in the collection of oral histories of camp liberators made this volume possible. He saw Dachau soon after its liberation and wanted the world to have no doubt as to its horrors and the reality of the Holocaust. I wish to thank Emory University, whose grant of the Fred J. Crawford Memorial Research Associateship enabled me to use the Witness to the Holocaust Collection with the thoroughness it deserves. At Emory I am indebted to Professors David Blumenthal and Jack Boozer for their support, and am particularly grateful for the day-to-day help and camaraderie of Kaethe Solomon and Terry Anderson. Without Terry's and Kaethe's aid, this book would not have seen the light of day. I also wish to thank Nancy Langford, whose contribution of duplicate transcripts made my life much easier. I might add that project volunteers at Emory too numerous to name have enriched this volume in many ways.

This book has also benefited greatly from the aid of those at the United States Army Military History Institute, in particular Drs. Richard Sommers and David Keogh. My first trip to Carlisle Barracks was funded by an Advanced Research Grant from the USAMHI, for which I have the pleasure of saying thank you. The staffs of the National Archives in Washington and the Records Office at Suitland, Maryland, have helped in my endeavors at those locations. In addition, those at the Defense Audio-Visual Agency helped me collect the large number of photographs needed for this volume. A special debt is owed to Stanley Falk, who had faith in this project and helped by opening doors and giving good advice.

Grants for research travel and time off from teaching are the life blood of scholarship, and here I have been extremely lucky. I thank the National Endowment for the Humanities for a Fellowship for Independent Study and Research which allowed me a year to do research and writing. I would like to thank the American Council of Learned Societies for a generous grant-in-aid that enabled me to do required research travel, including a trip to the sites of the concentration camps. I would also like to thank the University Research Institute of the University of Texas for its generous support in supplementing these grants.

Most of all, of course, I owe a central and great debt to those veterans who took the time to contribute their memories to the Witness to the Holocaust Project and to me personally. They themselves made history and I hope I have done them justice. I want to make special mention of the fact that although I could not use more than but a sampling of the Witness to the Holocaust interviews in the text, I greatly profited and was greatly moved by the entire collection.

Creating a book from manuscript pages and a set of photographs is no easy task, and for their guiding hand in this endeavor I especially thank Sheldon Meyer and Leona Capeless, as well as countless others at Oxford University Press. Finally I wish to thank my wife, Penne Restad, for expert editorial advice and unfailing support as I faced and tried to make sense of the frightening revelation that stands at the center of this book.

Sources

Central to my understanding of GI reactions were the interviews preserved on tape and in transcript at the Fred R. Crawford Witness to the Holocaust Project, Emory University, Atlanta, Georgia 30322. The Project has also published facsimile editions of various rare sources, including the pamphlets *Dachau* (Publication #2) and *The Seventy-First Came . . . to Gunskirchen Lager* (Publication #1) referred to in the text, as well as a reprint of the Congressional Committee Report, *Atrocities and Other Conditions in Concentration Camps in Germany* (Publication #3). It has recently reproduced an edition of *KZ* (Publication #5), another U.S. Army pamphlet meant to educate German citizens about the camps. These and other publications can be ordered directly from the Project at the address given above.

My special relationship with the Witness to the Holocaust Project allowed me to concentrate my oral history research on its collection of well over 125 interviews and scores of questionnaires, but future researchers should be aware that other major resources exist. In the first rank is the oral history work of the Center for Holocaust Studies in New York; the Center has published excerpts from a number of interviews in Yaffa Eliach and Brana Gurewitsch, *The Liberators: Eyewitness Accounts of the Liberation of Concentration Camps* (1981), available from the Center. One should also consult the Liberators Remembered Project, Boston University.

As for manuscript sources and official records, my chief resources have been the National Archives and the United States Army Military History Institute. The former contains, in its Modern Military Section, valuable records on the camps that were channeled through Supreme Headquarters Allied Expeditionary Forces (SHAEF). In Suitland, Maryland, records of the individual units that liberated the camps are to be found. In all cases, however, it should be noted that research on the camps in these sources is of the needle-in-haystack variety, with few if sometimes rich yields. After all, the camps were not major military objectives.

Of another order entirely are the materials in the manuscript division of the United States Army Military History Institute at Carlisle Barracks, Pennsylvania. This collection, strong on personal records and memorabilia, demands patient document-by-document search by one looking for material about the American encounter with the camps. Long hours provided some rich rewards for this book.

Photographic research became a painful journey through some very fine archives. The Witness to the Holocaust Project had a number of unusual holdings from private collections. The National Archives still picture collection provided those photographs of the camps released by the Office of War Information. The most extensive collection is to be found at the Defense Audio-Visual Agency in Washington, where one can peruse endless files of Signal Corps photographs. It was from the DAVA collection, most of all, that the illustrations for this book were drawn.

Secondary works on the liberations exist, though each has its problems. Michael Selzer's dramatic *Deliverance Day* (1978) recounts the liberation of Dachau through extensive interviews of participants, compressed and altered into fictional form. While one gets a vivid sense of the events, it is impossible in most cases to tell where the basic facts turn into fictional constructs. Nerin Gun's *The Day of the Americans* (1966), an account of the liberation and of life at Dachau from an ex-prisoner of the camp, is both fascinating and frustrating as a source because of its author's eccentricities. Derrick Sington's *Belsen Uncovered* (1946) is a moving and insightful first person account of conditions at Belsen. In a class by itself is Marcus J. Smith's *Dachau: The Harrowing of Hell*

(1972), which not only recounts the impressions of an American doctor on the scene but also reproduces important primary source material about the prisoner committees.

Standard works on American and Allied conceptions of and attitudes toward Nazi genocide and the camps during the war include Robert W. Ross's recent *So It Was True: The American Protestant Press and the Nazi Persecution of the Jews* (1980) and Walter Laqueur's pathbreaking *The Terrible Secret: Suppression of the Truth About Hitler's Final Solution* (1980). As for postwar issues concerning the DPs, the best place to start is Leonard Dinnerstein's thorough-going *America and the Survivors of the Holocaust* (1982); see also Abram L. Sachar's *The Redemption of the Unwanted: From the Liberation of the Death Camps to the Founding of Israel* (1983). Some recent works about the American occupation of Germany that bear on the questions raised in this book include: Earl F. Ziemke, *The U.S. Army in the Occupation of Germany, 1944-46* (1975); Edward N. Peterson, *The American Occupation of Germany: Retreat to Victory* (1978); and, most recently, James F. Tent, *Mission on the Rhine: Reeducation and Denazification in American-Occupied Germany* (1982).

For the histories of the camps themselves, there is no better place to start than Konnilyn G. Feig's *Hitler's Death Camps: The Sanity of Madness* (1979), which in almost encyclopedic fashion covers the major and some of the minor camps and raises important questions about our vision of Nazi genocide. Works about individual camps are cited in my footnotes, and more extensive listings of sources can be found in Feig's bibliography. Two good and widely available works on Holocaust history are Lucy Dawidowicz, *The War Against the Jews* (1975) and Raul Hilberg, *The Destruction of the European Jews* (1967), and a recent proliferation of fine monographs too numerous to mention here await the interested reader. Finally, some works bear on a subject of importance to my larger concerns and a theme of the present volume: the difficulty of comprehending horrors as enormous as those found in the camps. I have looked at aspects of this problem through historical sources. Books that have contributed to our understanding of the problem through literary and other artistic sources include: Lawrence L. Langer, *The Holocaust and the Literary Imagination* (1975) and *Versions of Survival: The Holocaust and the Human Spirit* (1982); Terrence des Pres, *The Survivor: An Anatomy of Life in the Death Camps* (1976); Sidra DeKoven Ezrahi, *By Words Alone: The Holocaust in Literature* (1980); Lucy Dawidowicz, *The Holocaust and the Historians* (1981); and, most recently, Annette Insdorf, *Indelible Shadows: Film and the Holocaust* (1983).

Notes

Abbreviations for frequently cited sources:

Witness to the Holocaust: The Fred R. Crawford Witness to the Holocaust Project, Emory University, Atlanta, Georgia.

USAMHI: United States Army Military History Institute, Carlisle Barracks, Pennsylvania.

Preface

1. Alfred Kazin, *Starting Out in the Thirties* (Boston, 1965), 166.
2. The phrase "Hun atrocities" was actually used by a liberator of Mauthausen to describe his notions of the camps before he actually entered one. See *The Seventy-First Came . . . to Gunskirchen Lager* (n.p., 1945, reprinted as Witness to the Holocaust Publication Series #1, Emory University, Atlanta, 1979), 18.

Chapter 1

1. The most convenient summary of the history of Natzwiller is to be found in Konnilyn G. Feig, *Hitler's Death Camps: The Sanity of Madness* (New York, 1979), 215-26.
2. CBS World News broadcast, August 18, 1940, tape used in possession of Audio-Visual Archives, USAMHI.
3. See Richard Lauderback, "Sunday in Poland," *Life,* Sept. 18, 1944, 17; Edgar Snow, "Here the Nazi Butchers Wasted Nothing: Nazi Murder Factory," *Saturday Evening Post,* Oct. 28, 1944. On how much was known in the West and when, see Walter Laqueur, *The Terrible Secret: Suppression of the Truth About Hitler's "Final Solution"* (Boston, 1980), *passim.*

4. Milton Bracker, "Alsace Nazi Prison Neat and Efficient," *New York Times,* Dec. 5, 1944, 7. Quotations from Bracker in following paragraphs are from the same source. A few weeks later the *Times* ran a pictorial of the camp, showing scenes similar to those encountered by Bracker. See "The Lublin of Alsace: The Nazi Order As It Operated in France," *ibid.,* Dec. 18, 1944, 3.

5. "Concentration Camp at NATZWILLER [*sic*]," RG 331, Records of Allied Operational and Occupation Headquarters, WWII, SHAEF/G-5/ 2717, Modern Military, National Archives, Washington, D.C.

6. See Loren Carroll to Douglas MacArthur II, n.d. [April 1945], Alben Barkley Mss., University of Kentucky Library, Lexington, for evidence that this doubting of the French was a widespread problem.

7. "Nazi Atrocities," in George H. Gallup, *The Gallup Poll: Public Opinion, 1935-1971* (New York, 1972), I (1935-48), 472.

8. Interview of John Glustrom, Witness to the Holocaust Collection, Emory University.

9. See, for instance, any number of quotations cited in Robert W. Ross, *So It Was True: The American Protestant Press and the Nazi Persecution of the Jews* (Minneapolis, 1980), *passim.*

10. Laqueur, *The Terrible Secret,* 236-37.

11. Armin L. Robinson, ed., *The Ten Commandments: Ten Short Novels of Hitler's War Against the Moral Code* (New York, 1943).

12. *Ibid.,* 71-116 and especially 109-16.

13. Anne Seghers, *The Seventh Cross* (Boston, 1942); the motion picture was released in 1944.

14. Reinhold Niebuhr, "Jews After the War, I," *The Nation,* Feb. 21, 1942, 214.

15. Meyer Levin, *In Search: An Autobiography* (New York, 1950), 232.

Chapter 2

1. Meyer Levin, *In Search: An Autobiography,* 231-32 and for paragraph that follows.

2. Charles B. McDonald, *The Last Offensive* (Washington, 1973), 376-78.

3. Interview of Joseph Kushlis, Witness to the Holocaust.

4. Interview of Frank Hamburger, Witness to the Holocaust.

5. Colonel Charles R. Codman, *Drive* (Boston, 1957), 281-82; Omar N. Bradley, *A Soldier's Story* (New York, 1951), 539; see also, Diary of Chester B. Hansen, April 12, 1945, and diary of Hobart A. Gay, April 12, 1945, both in manuscript division, USAMHI.

6. Bradley, *A Soldier's Story,* 539; Charles R. Codman, *Drive,* 282.

7. *Ibid.,* 283; for similar senses of Eisenhower's reaction, see diary of Chester B. Hansen, April 12, 1945, and diary of Hobart A. Gay, April 12, 1945, both in manuscript division, USAMHI.

8. Cable reprinted in *Atrocities and Other Conditions in Concentration Camps in Germany . . . ,* 79th Congress, 1st Session, Senate Document No. 47 (Washington, 1945, reprinted as Witness to the Holocaust Publication Series #3, 1983), 1.

9. Feig, *Hitler's Death Camps,* 227-33.
10. Al Newman, "Nordhausen: A Hell Factory Worked by the Living Dead," *Newsweek,* April 23, 1945, 51.
11. "Interview with Col. D. B. Hardin, G-5, VII Corps, Nordhausen, Germany. 14 April 1945. Interviewed by 1st Lt. George E. Moise, 2nd Info and Hist Sv, VII Corps, First US Army," Record Group No. 407, Combat Interviews, Interview #346A, Box 24113, National Archives, Suitland, Maryland.
12. Interview of C. W. Doughty, Witness to the Holocaust.
13. Interview of William B. Lovelady, Witness to the Holocaust.
14. Interview of Fred Bohm, Witness to the Holocaust.
15. *Ibid.*
16. Interview of C. W. Doughty, Witness to the Holocaust.
17. Robert J. Lifton, *Death in Life: Survivors of Hiroshima* (New York, 1967), 31-34 and *passim;* interview of C. W. Doughty, Witness to the Holocaust.
18. Newman, "Nordhausen: A Hell Factory . . . ," 51.
19. Interview of Morris Parloff, Witness to the Holocaust.
20. *Ibid.*

Chapter 3

1. Percy Knauth, *Germany in Defeat* (New York, 1946), 30-31; Knauth, "Buchenwald," *Time,* April 30, 1945, 40, 43.
2. For a good summary treatment of Buchenwald, see Feig, *Hitler's Death Camps,* 85-115.
3. For an account of the nature of the Communist faction and its sources of power, see Egon W. Fleck and Edward A Tenenbaum, "Buchenwald: A Preliminary Report, 24 April 1945," in RG 331, SHAEF/G-5/2711/7.21, National Archives, Washington, D.C.; for an anti-Communist account of prisoner resistance efforts by a resistance leader, see Christopher Burney, *The Dungeon Democracy* (New York, 1946).
4. See Fleck and Tenenbaum, "Buchenwald: A Preliminary Report, 24 April 1945."
5. *Ibid.;* and Christopher Burney, *The Dungeon Democracy,* 117-39.
6. This account relies on information from letter of Pierre C. T. Verheye to George Hoffman [*sic*], Dec. 7, 1972; typewritten transcript of letter of Colonel Robert J. Bennett to Pierre C. T. Verheye, Nov. 5, 1972; and After Action Report for Combat Team 9 (9th Armored Infantry Battalion), CCA, 6th Armored Division, 25 March-17 April 1945, all in The Armor—U.S.—6th Division Papers (The George Hofmann Collection), manuscript division, USAMHI.
7. Interview of Kenneth Bowers, Witness to the Holocaust.
8. Interview of Fred Mercer, Witness to the Holocaust.
9. Interview of John Glustrom, Witness to the Holocaust.
10. Fleck and Tenenbaum, "Buchenwald: A Preliminary Report, 24 April 1945," 13-14.
11. Percy Knauth, *Germany in Defeat,* 38-39.

12. *Ibid.*
13. *Ibid.*
14. Margaret Bourke-White, *"Dear Fatherland, Rest Quietly": A Report on the Collapse of Hitler's "Thousand Years"* (New York, 1946), 73; Margaret Bourke-White, *Portrait of Myself* (New York, 1963), 259. See also John Eisenhower's reaction to seeing Buchenwald as described in John S. D. Eisenhower, *Strictly Personal* (New York, 1974), 89-90.
15. Fleck and Tenenbaum, "Buchenwald: A Preliminary Report 24 April 1945," 14.
16. Meyer Levin, *In Search,* 240-44.

Chapter 4

1. James M. Gavin, *On to Berlin: Battles of an Airborne Commander 1943-46* (New York, 1978), 288-89; David Rousset, *The Other Kingdom* (New York, 1947), 160-62.
2. Interview of Samuel Glasshow, Witness to the Holocaust.
3. Interview of J. D. Digilio, Witness to the Holocaust.
4. Interview of Samuel Glasshow, Witness to the Holocaust.
5. *Ibid.*
6. James M. Gavin, *On to Berlin,* 289.
7. Interview of David Campbell, Witness to the Holocaust.
8. *Ibid.*
9. Daniel Camous, "Report on the Atrocity Camp of Tekla (Leipzig), April 24, 1945," in WWII Miscellany, Eaton File.
10. This account is based on various sources but can be most easily consulted in Bill Walton, "Erla," *Time,* April 30, 1945.
11. Margaret Bourke-White, *"Dear Fatherland, Rest Quietly,"* 77-79.
12. Letter of April 27, 1945, WWII Miscellany, Eaton File.
13. *Ibid.*
14. "Flossenburg: The Story of One Concentration Camp," *National Jewish Monthly,* Oct. 1945, 45-46; see also Feig, *Hitler's Death Camps,* 129-32, for more background on Flossenburg.
15. For background on Belsen, see *ibid.,* 370-93; for an extraordinary account of the British experience at the camp, see Derrick Sington, *Belsen Uncovered* (London, 1946).
16. Interview of Curtis Mitchell, Witness to the Holocaust, and narrative of Mitchell in "The Valley of Death, the Armies of Life," *Moment* May 1981, 14, 17-19.
17. *Ibid.*
18. *Ibid.,* 19.

Chapter 5

1. Karl Baedeker, *Southern Germany: Wurtemberg and Bavaria, Handbook for Travellers* (Leipzig and London, 1914), 303; Marcus J. Smith, *Dachau: The Harrowing of Hell* (Albuquerque, 1972), 79.

2. Paul Berben, *Dachau: 1933-1945, The Official History* (London, 1975), 1-19, 123-37, and *passim*.

3. *Ibid.*, 96-101.

4. Interview of Bill Allison, Witness to the Holocaust.

5. Interview of Jack Hallett, Witness to the Holocaust.

6. Interview of Henry DeJarnette, Witness to the Holocaust. For various accounts of these skirmishes and the American entry into the camp, see Charles R. McDonald, *The Last Offensive* (Washington, 1973), 436; Nerin E. Gun, *The Day of the Americans* (New York, 1966), 55-66; Michael Selzer, *Deliverance Day: The Last Hours at Dachau* (Philadelphia, 1978), 160-97; see also the combat narratives of each division in RG 407 342-INF-222-03 and RG 407 345-INF-157-03 (Both April, 1945), National Archives, Suitland, Maryland.

7. Interview of John Dunn, Witness to the Holocaust; Frederick F. Lyons, "My Visit to Dachau—Notorious Nazi Prison Camp," typescript in The Infantry—100th Division Collection, USAMHI. Lyons contributed a scrapbook of his visit to Dachau, and in it is a photograph of the bodies he saw. A caption reads: "On close observation the face of a beautiful girl can be seen where indicated by an arrow, in the midst of emaciated male bodies."

8. Interview of Jack Hallett, Witness to the Holocaust; see account of massacre in Selzer, *Deliverance Day*, 186-92.

9. Interview of Jack Hallett, Witness to the Holocaust.

10. Interview of "anonymous" liberator, Witness to the Holocaust.

11. This account is based on Felix Sparks's version of the events, which seems to be sound in its essentials. See Sparks's story in "Dachau and Its Liberation," typescript bulletin of the "157th Infantry Association," 20 March 1984.

12. The aftermath of the affair is worth recounting. Some weeks after V-E Day, with the 157th Infantry Regiment now on occupation duty in Munich, Sparks was told that General Linden was attempting to make good on his court-martial threat and General Frederick advised him to leave quietly for the United States while he handled the matter. Sparks was given a command car and made it as far as Le Havre, where an MP informed him that he was under arrest. The MP said that he would escort him back to Seventh Army headquarters in Bavaria. Sparks told the MP that he would not submit to arrest, but would voluntarily get back to headquarters. "Glancing around at my three men casually standing by with loaded rifles," as Sparks tells it, "he agreed to my proposal." When he arrived he reported to General Patton. The General informed him that some serious charges had been made. Sparks told him the story. According to Sparks, Patton paused and then said: "There is no point in an explanation. I have already had these charges investigated and they are a bunch of crap. I'm going to tear up these goddamn papers on you and your men." And that was that. This account, *ibid*.

13. The question of the gas chamber is a matter of controversy even today. The official position of those who run the Dachau memorial is that it was built as an extermination gas chamber in 1942 but never actually

used. See Berben, *Dachau: The Official History, 1933-1945,* 8. At the same time, many survivors swear that it was used. For instance, see Nerin Gun, *The Day of the Americans,* 67-68, 129, and photographs opposite page 129. Marcus Smith got all different versions when he was there. See Marcus J. Smith, *Dachau: The Harrowing of Hell,* 94-95, 108.

14. Seventh Army, *Dachau* (n.p., 1945, reprinted as Witness to the Holocaust Publication Series #2, 1982), 22-26. A reprint of this pamphlet is available from the Witness to the Holocaust Project, Emory University, Atlanta, Georgia 30322.
15. *Ibid.,* 26.

Chapter 6

1. Evelyn Le Chene, *Mauthausen: The History of a Death Camp* (London, 1971), 19-25.
2. *Ibid.,* 26-33.
3. *Ibid.,* 34-132.
4. *Ibid.,* 65-66.
5. *Ibid.,* 199-256.
6. See, *ibid.,* 139-59, and Raul Hilberg, *The Destruction of the European Jews* (New York, 1961), 509-54.
7. LeChene, *Mauthausen,* 178-98.
8. *Ibid.,* 199-242.
9. *Ibid.,* 199-256.
10. Interview of George E. King, Witness to the Holocaust.
11. *Ibid.*
12. Interview of Franklin Lee Clark, Witness to the Holocaust.
13. *The Seventy-First Came . . . to Gunskirchen Lager.*
14. Quoted in Le Chene, *Mauthausen,* 147.
15. Capt. J. D. Pletcher, "The Americans Have Come — At Last," in *The Seventy-First Came . . . to Gunskirchen Lager.*
16. Interview of Bert Weston, Witness to the Holocaust.

Chapter 7

1. Percy Knauth, "Buchenwald," *Time,* April 30, 1945, 43.
2. Cable reprinted in *Atrocities and Other Conditions in Concentration Camps in Germany . . .-, .*
3. *Ibid.,* 16.
4. See, for instance, James F. Byrnes to Barkley, May 25, 1945, and Alben Barkley to James F. Byrnes, June 1, 1945, in Alben W. Barkley Papers, University of Kentucky Library, Lexington.
5. Manuscript of Vorys speech, in various parts, "Inspecting the Concentration Camps" and "The Three Camps," in Mss 280, Box 85, Vorys Papers, Archives Library, Ohio Historical Society, Columbus.
6. Omaha *World-Herald,* May 23, 1945, p. 4, col. 3.
7. Joseph Pulitzer, *A Report to the American People* (St. Louis, 1945), 94.
8. *Ibid.,* 9.

9. The most convenient source for the review is James Agee, *Agee on Film I* (New York, 1958), 161-62.
10. Pulitzer, *A Report to the American People,* 16-17.
11. Milton Mayer, "Let the Swiss Do It!", *The Progressive,* May 14, 1945.
12. Interview of Bert Weston, Witness to the Holocaust.
13. Interview of Jack Hallett, Witness to the Holocaust.
14. Interview of Philip Carlquist, Witness to the Holocaust.
15. Interview of Joseph Kushlis, Witness to the Holocaust.
16. Bradley to ETOUSA, SHAEF/G-5/2711/7.21, National Archives, Washington, D.C.
17. "Nazi War Crimes," in George H. Gallup, *The Gallup Poll: Public Opinion, 1935-1971,* I (1935-48), 504.
18. Alfred Kazin, *Starting Out in the Thirties,* 166; Susan Sontag, *On Photography* (New York, 1977), 19-20.

Chapter 8

1. S. R. Michelsen to Donald R. Heath, "Conditions at the Mauthausen Concentration Camp, Austria," June 8, 1945, SHAEF/G-5/DP/2711/7, National Archives, Washington, D.C.; M. J. Proudfoot to Executive Displaced Persons Branch, G-5, "Memorandum No. 1: Concentration Camp at Mauthausen, Austria, *ibid.;* Warren F. Draper to Assistant Chief of Staff, G-5, SHAEF, "Report of Visit to Buchenwald Concentration Camp near Weimar, Germany, 25 April 1945 . . . .", April 30, 1945, *ibid.;* S. R. Michelsen to Assistant Chief of Staff, G-5 Division, "Visit to German Concentration Camp at Dachau," 19 May 1945, and J. D. Faulkner and V. R. Paravicini to Displaced Persons Branch, G-5 Division, SHAEF, "Report on Field Trip to 6 Army Group Areas," both, *ibid.*
2. C. I. Shottland and M. MacDonald to Executive, Displaced Persons Branch, G-5, "Report on Field Trip to Buchenwald, 8/9 June 1945," 12 June 1945, *ibid.*
3. A sensitive appraisal of such problems is to be found in Sington, *Belsen Uncovered,* 145-76.
4. For Jewish service incident, see Selzer, *Deliverance Day,* 220-26; for more general senses of internal strife and work of the International Committee at Dachau, see Marcus J. Smith, *Dachau: The Harrowing of Hell,* 155-77, 202-14.
5. The most recent and best work to attempt to put some order on the displaced persons problem is Leonard Dinnerstein, *America and the Survivors of the Holocaust* (New York, 1982), especially in the first two chapters.
6. *Ibid.,* 13-24.
7. *Ibid.,* 11-12.
8. *Ibid.,* chap. 1; see also interview of Rabbi Judah Nadich, Witness to the Holocaust; Nadich was Eisenhower's adviser on Jewish affairs at the time.
9. Dinnerstein, *America and the Survivors of the Holocaust,* 13.

10. *Ibid.,* 21, for evidence that Balt camps became showcases for the DP policy.
11. *Ibid.* chap. 1; and Irving Heymont, *Among the Survivors of the Holocaust—1945: The Landsberg DP Camp Letters of Major Irving Heymont, United States Army* (Cincinnati, 1982), *passim.*
12. Richard Joseph and Waverly Root, "Why So Many GIs Like the Germans Best," *Reader's Digest,* March 1946, 5-6 and *passim.*
13. *Ibid.*
14. Captain C. E. Jack, "DPS VS. GERMAN AUTHORITIES," 8 July 1945, Hq DP 8, 2nd ECA Regiment to AC of S, G-5, XII Corps, in the World War II Miscellaneous Collection: Robertson, USAMHI.
15. Patton Diary, Oct. 1, 1945, in Martin Blumenson, ed., *The Patton Papers, 1940-1945* (Boston, 1974), 787-88; *America and Survivors of the Holocaust,* 15.
16. *Ibid.,* in order, 750, 744, 766.
17. *Ibid.,* in order, 759, 788, 754.
18. "Reported Riot at DIESSEN and LANDSBERG DP Camps," 29 April 1946, in Martin M. Phillipsborn Papers, USAMHI.
19. Pat Frank, "Patton Turned Back 600 Jews Fleeing Terror in Poland," clipping from *New York Post,* n.d., 1945, in Ernest N. Harmon Papers, USAMHI.
20. *Ibid.*
21. Colonel John H. Fye, "Memorandum, To: Commanding General, in re letter from the American Ambassador and enclosure thereto from World Jewish Congress dated 21 September 1945," in Ernest N. Harmon Papers, USAMHI.
22. "Report of Earl G. Harrison," reprinted in complete form as Appendix B of Dinnerstein, *America and the Survivors of the Holocaust,* 291-305.
23. *Ibid.,* 293.
24. *Ibid.,* 294-97.
25. *Ibid.,* 298-304.
26. *Ibid.,* 304-5.
27. Reprint of Army Talk in Dinnerstein, *America and the Survivors of the Holocaust,* 307-13, quotes from 313.
28. Irving Heymont, letter of 19 Sept. 1945, in *Among the Survivors of the Holocaust—1945,* 5.
29. Letters of 2, 4, and 8 Oct. 1945, *ibid.,* 30-40, 44-5.
30. Letters of 18 and 20 Oct. 1945, *ibid.,* 60, 63.
31. *Ibid.,* 109-11.
32. Interview of Howard Margol, Witness to the Holocaust.

Epilogue

1. *New York Times,* April 21, 1945, p. 5, col. 7.; see Susan Sontag, *On Photography,* 20-21, for a different treatment of some of the same ideas presented in this and the paragraphs following.

Index

(Page numbers in italic indicate photographs)

188

190